Love *Is My* Only Master

Spiritual Reflections
and
Affirmations
for the
Heart and Soul

Love is My Only Master provides uplifting thoughts for every day. These reflections for the heart and soul are to be planted in your mind and heart each morning as you arise. These seeds of nourishment will help expand the light within and will assist you in affirming the loving presence of spirit in your soul and the awesome working of Spirit in your life.

In the pages of this book, Kathryn Peters presents a very easy to read and absorb format of thought stimuli and affirmations that can provide that oasis of inspirational renewal in just a few moments reading.

Dr. Paul Leon Masters
Founder & President, The University of Metaphysics

Also by Kathryn M. Peters
HeartLights: Affirmation deck for Divination

LOVE

is my

only

MASTER

*Spiritual Reflections
and
Affirmations
for the
Heart and Soul*

By
Kathryn M. Peters

HeartLight Productions

HeartLight Productions
2161 W. Williams, Suite 236
Fallon, Nevada 89406

First Quality Paperback Edition 1993
Copyright © 1993, Kathryn M. Peters
Compiled and edited by Michelene K. Bell

Cover and text designed by Tracy L. Panzarella
Co-publisher, Greg Nielsen, Conscious Books 1-800-322-9943

10 9 8 7 6 5 4 3 2 1

Library of Congress Catalog Card Number: 93-093587

ISBN 0-9638490-0-X

Printed and Bound in the United States of America

Dedication

My Sweet Mother,

I dedicate this book to you. God *filled* me with the spirit of Love, but only you taught me *how* to Love. Thanks Mom.

Acknowledgments

To Uriel and Mylonka, as your channel I have found my peace and my purpose.

I want to extend my heartfelt appreciation to my family for enduring my endless preoccupation during the gestation of this project. And I thank them each for choosing to be a part of my life and for the lessons they have volunteered to help me learn.

James Robert -
You have taught me the realities of unconditional love and you have seen to it that my every dream came true.

Elizabeth Michelle -
By watching you step so gracefully into your magnificence, you gave me the courage to believe in myself.

Alixandra Dorian-
You are a wonder! You have inspired me to never stop reaching for the unreachable.

Evan Jameson -
Your shining eyes, beautiful smile and kind heart create a magic that has changed my life forever.

Alysia Kathryn -
You are an exquisite combination of joy and fire. I am so glad we share a birthday, a name and a lifetime of love.

Angelica Arielle -
The incredible beauty of your being is proof positive that angels do indeed live among us.

Andriana Nicholette -
Welcome darling one. You have fortified my soul by your presence, and blessed me with another opportunity to love.

Michelene K. Bell -
Sis, I thank you for you eternal love and tireless efforts on my behalf. Without you, and *In Light Times,* this project would would have never been. Goddess, bless you, always.

Tracy L. Panzarella -
You have an extra special kind of light about you. Tracy, I thank you for bringing it into my life along with you creative vision, your immense talent and your frienship.

Greg Nielsen -
There is no one quite like you, and I knew that the moment we met. I thank you from the bottom of my heart for sharing your genius and for being my guide and mentor on this project. Greggie, you're the best!

♥ ─────────

Introduction

Some years ago, I found myself in a rather serious conversation with my oldest and dearest friend, Lacy Moore. As I recall, I was bemoaning the state of my life with unusual zest when Lacy said to me, "Kathryn, if you want to change your world, change your master." The impact of those words have never left me. From that time on, I determined that love would be my only master, and that I would no longer allow anything to usurp the power of love in my life. For only love makes life worth living.

This book is an outgrowth of the power of love. Because I desired to increase the love I gave and received each and every day, I created a monthly column entitled, *Daily Light Seeds*, which appeared in Michelene Bell's wonderful periodical, *In Light Times.*

The *Daily Light Seeds,* were designed to expand the heart and soul's capacity to embrace and embody the light of spirit. Daily activities and mundane thoughts become spiritual acts of devotion when the human heart is functioning at the proper frequency. The *Daily Light Seeds* originally appeared pretty much the same as they do in this book. They are a spiritual reflection and affirmation coupled to form a seed of positive, spiritual light which, when nurtured, will take root in your life.

Well, the *Daily Light Seeds* became quite popular and soon I was receiving calls and letters from admirers of my work. Many encouraged me to publish the *Daily Light Seeds* in book form, and here it is!

It is my deepest hope that you, dear reader, will be enriched by the reflections and affirmations found within these pages. We all must learn to live our spirituality, not just talk about it. The application of spiritual principles in everyday life is often challenging. Yet, with a little help from **"Love *is My Only* Master"**, living in the Divine Presence of Love can become a beautiful reality for us all.

September 22, 1993
In the Radiance of Love,
I Am
Kathryn

Table of Contents

H

I

J

K

L

M

N

R

S

♥

♥

V

♥

W

How To Use This Book

As the flaming sun dawns each morning, life deserves to be celebrated anew. By avowing to consciously focus our thoughts and actions on the qualities of Spirit, we show reverence for the life within and surrounding us. *Daily Light Seeds* are to be planted in your mind and heart each morning as you begin your day, and again each evening, as your day draws to an end. If this is done with sincerity and regularity, these seeds will assist you in affirming the loving presence of Spirit in your soul and the awesome workings of Spirit in your life.

The *Daily Light Seeds* may be meditated upon in order, as they appear in the book, or you may use your intuition to find the light seed best suited to your needs at any particular moment. This is done by silently embracing a thought or question. Then, simply allow the book to open naturally. The page your eyes falls upon, first, will offer you either the guidance you are seeking, or the wisdom that you have forgotten.

Dear friends, I offer these spiritual reflections and affirmations to you as seeds of motivation and inspiration. Thoughts are power. The thoughts we hold dearest will manifest in our lives, without fail, for better or worse. So allow yourself the pleasure of beautiful thoughts, as you turn the pages of this book, open your heart to the Voice of Spirit, and open your life to the Miracle of Love.

♥

DISCIPLESHIP

My spiritual beliefs ask that I follow a
path of goodness and live a life of love.
Being dedicated to that end is the
heart and soul of my mission on Earth.

♥ ## AFFIRMATION ♥

"I am a Spiritual Disciple, love is my only master."

LOVE *is my only* MASTER

1

Today
I plant the seed of…

MY SPIRITUAL SELF-PORTRAIT

If placed before a blank canvas and asked to create my self-portrait, how would I look? Would I draw my eyes too small or too large, or would I see and convey the shining Light of Spirit behind them? As I consider the way in which I see myself, first I must view my eternal self through the unerring eyes of Mother Goddess.

❤ **AFFIRMATION** ❤

"As only a mother can, the Goddess has seen my perfection from the beginning of time."

LOVE *is my only* MASTER

─────────────────── ♥ ───────────────────

Today
I plant the seed of…

HIGHER CONSCIOUSNESS

It has been said that if I knock, the door
will be opened. Today I will knock upon
the door of Higher Mind, for I wish to think
the thoughts of Spirit. And, I shall knock
once more, for I yearn to know the Peace
of God.

♥ **AFFIRMATION** ♥

**"The entrance to Higher Consciousness
shall be made visible when I approach
it with a sincere heart and an open mind."**

LOVE *is my only* MASTER

Today
I plant the seed of…

PRAYER

There have been times in my life when I could not reach clarity or serenity of being no matter how often I meditated, or how hard I tried. It is in these times of isolation that I must ask for the Vision of Heaven. In other words, I must pray.

♥ AFFIRMATION ♥

"Through heartfelt prayer I give the Holy Spirit permission to cleanse my heart, clear my mind and heal my spirit."

LOVE *is my only* MASTER

♥

LOVING SERVITUDE

Through every act of loving kindness and every word of encouragement I give to my fellow souls of Light. I am acting in loving servitude to Almighty Spirit. Above all else, I have come to Earth to be of service to the Family of God.

♥ **AFFIRMATION** ♥

"Each day and in every moment, I vow to lovingly serve the One and Only Great Spirit of Love."

LOVE *is my only* MASTER

---❤---

THE SIGNIFICANCE OF LIFE

I am not upon this Earth simply to dream of and strive for the day, out yonder, when my soul is finally freed from the physical realm. Life is a magical journey in and of itself. It is a quest for love, discovery and celebration. If it is life eternal that I seek, let me step into eternity today.

❤   **AFFIRMATION**   ❤

"The true significance of life is found in the very moment I am living."

LOVE *is my only* MASTER

Today
I plant the seed of...

DISCERNING ANGELS

My angels are the Guardians of my Light in this realm of shadow. Angels are present to instill hope, respond to prayer and affirmation along with overseeing my progress upon the Emerald Sphere. Acknowledging the presence and power of angels in my life is the first step I will take towards establishing a lifelong love affair with miracles.

♥ **AFFIRMATION** ♥

"My dear Angels of Mercy, I call upon you this day to assist me in discerning your presence and accepting your help."

LOVE *is my only* MASTER

♥

RIGHT MINDFULNESS

In a single day, I am bombarded from all directions by rumors of war and tales of humanity's inhumanity. In addition, my personal world is filled with endless demands to meet, as well as, countless responsibilities to shoulder. In order to successfully maneuver my way through all of this, to the Peace of God, I must maintain right mindfulness.

♥ **AFFIRMATION** ♥

"When I can recognize the presence and power of Divinity in each and every life experience, I am successfully maintaining right mindfulness."

LOVE *is my only* MASTER

8

Today
I plant the seed of...

THE VIRTUE OF PATIENCE

Once I become cognizant of the creative power given to me by the presence of the Indwelling Christ, I need also become cognizant of the Divine mandate for patience. I create my own reality, yet the manifestation of that reality is not always according to my personal timing. The Universe oversees my life and delivers my highest good in a moment of perfection.

♥   **AFFIRMATION**   ♥

**"By cultivating the virtue of patience,
I manifest my faith in the perfection of the Universe."**

LOVE *is my only* MASTER

Today
I plant the seed of...

LOOKING BEYOND APPEARANCES

Within my daily life there are often unsettling situations that arise, which leave me feeling disturbed or resentful. When this happens, it is to my best advantage if I can train myself to look beyond the appearance of injustice, inconvenience or disagreement. With a little practice I will begin to see that just under the surface of every apparent adversity lies the seed of my future joy.

♥   **AFFIRMATION**   ♥

"It is only my judgement of a situation that blinds me from seeing the endless good that lies just beyond its appearance."

LOVE *is my only* MASTER

Today
I plant the seed of...

FLOWING WITH SPIRIT

Life on Earth is a material projection of Spirit's Holy Imagination. The cosmic stream of consciousness flows on course, ever steady, ever strong. As an individuation of Spirit, I am one with the flow of life. I am inseparable from the flow of Spirit.

♥   **AFFIRMATION**   ♥

"My soul recognizes only tranquility and my heart experiences only love when I am aligned with the flow of Spirit."

LOVE *is my only* MASTER

Today
I plant the seed of…

TAPPING INTO PAST LIVES

All that I am this moment, is the culmination of all that I have been over the course of many lifetimes. Understanding my past assists me in making the most of my present. Moreover, the key to my future may well be awaiting me in an ancient memory stored in my eternal soul.

❤ **AFFIRMATION** ❤

"Tapping into my past lives enables me to make tremendous strides upon the path of self-understanding and unfoldment."

LOVE *is my only* MASTER

♥

Today
I plant the seed of…

FINDING MY PURPOSE

Why am I here? What is it that I have to offer the world? How many times I have asked these questions, fully expecting the voice of Heaven to answer me? Yet, the answers are so obvious, if only I have eyes to see! What am I good at? What is it that I really enjoy doing that also brings joy to others? Once I have answered these questions, I will know, without a doubt, why I am here.

♥ **AFFIRMATION** ♥

**"To find my purpose I need look no further
than the desires of my heart."**

LOVE *is my only* MASTER

♥

INNER WISDOM

The information and knowledge needed to help me successfully champion my life cannot be ascertained through external sources. Without fail, on a daily basis, I need to turn Inward. I need to enter the silence of holy reverence. Within the silence, I will receive the inner wisdom that is available to me and can only be transmitted through my Indwelling Christ.

♥ **AFFIRMATION** ♥

"My inner wisdom speaks in the language of Infinite Love."

LOVE *is my only* MASTER

14

---------------- ♥ ----------------

RECEIVING MY GOOD

Life is good. Once I accept this at a soul level, I open myself to receive the full goodness of life on earth. Despite the appearance of poverty and despair, I will receive an endless bounty of blessings from Spirit, if it is here that I keep my mind focused.

♥   **AFFIRMATION**   ♥

"As a child of Divinity, I am entitled to receive only the best of everything in my life."

LOVE *is my only* MASTER

---- ♥ ----

REMAINING CORRECT

As I am learning to allow myself to be swept uphill by the *increases* of life's unending flow, I need also pay attention to the way in which I conduct myself in times of inevitable *decrease*. In remaining correct, I am asked by the Universe to act as a noble champion of spiritual ideals, regardless of any challenges facing me.

♥ **AFFIRMATION** ♥

"I am a Spiritual Warrior dedicated to remaining correct to all Divine Principles."

LOVE *is my only* MASTER

♥

ASTROLOGY

Almost two millennia ago, the ancient astrologers foretold the coming of the Prince of Peace by looking into the Face of Heaven and interpreting her signs. This art remains as valid and as invaluable a tool for self-discovery today as it was to the seers and prophets of antiquity. A sincere desire to learn the basics of astrology will serve to accelerate my spiritual self-unfoldment.

AFFIRMATION

♥ ♥

**"When I look to the stars
I behold the many faces of God."**

LOVE *is my only* MASTER

17

Today
I plant the seed of...

TRANSFORMATION

As a worker of light, I have come to planet Earth to offer my assistance to the salvation of this beauteous orb and her children. Along the way, I have chosen to learn a few personal lessons also. As I habitually keep my mind on Spirit, regardless of the circumstances challenging me to grow, I transcend the Earth's consciousness. Thusly, I facilitate the transformation of the human vibration.

♥ **AFFIRMATION** ♥

**"A transformation of my thinking
transforms the world."**

LOVE *is my only* MASTER

Today
I plant the seed of...

BELIEVING IN MAGIC

To truly be alive is to be open to the real magic that exists within my soul. Magic surrounds me like the warmth of a mother's hug. The magic in giving and receiving love fills me with unlimited potential. The magic of believing in myself turns that potential into the reality of my true being.

♥ **AFFIRMATION** ♥

"When I learn to believe in magic, the Gates of Heaven open wide and shower my life with enchantment from the inside out."

LOVE *is my only* MASTER

Today
I plant the seed of...

TEACHING

I need not be an Ascended Master before Spirit sees me as a teacher. Each and every set back and success in my life that have caused me to move a little closer to Infinite Truth, has prepared me as a spiritual teacher. Sharing with others my personal truth is the most beautiful way on Earth for me to teach the fullness of life.

♥ ## AFFIRMATION ♥

"As I share the love and light I have experienced, I teach the Love of God."

LOVE *is my only* MASTER

Today
I plant the seed of...

UNBURDENING MY HEART

I have declared my Divinity for all of Heaven and Earth to hear. Now I need to unburden my heart of all the resentment, envy, guilt and anger that I have allowed to accumulate there over the past year. Today, let me begin my life anew with a cheerful disposition and an unburdened heart.

♥   **AFFIRMATION**   ♥

"Divine Love will be magnetically drawn to my heart when it has been emptied of all malice."

LOVE *is my only* MASTER

Today
I plant the seed of...

WALKING MY TALK

If I had time to digest the wisdom con-
tained in every metaphysical volume
ever written, not one word of it would
benefit me, unless I could put those
words of wisdom into practical, daily
application. To be well read is to be
nothing more than an educated fool
without the ability to walk the talk.

♥ **AFFIRMATION** ♥

**"Dear One, my heart fills with joy when I
know I am being faithful to your word."**

LOVE *is my only* MASTER

♥

SAYING YES TO LIFE

Life asks that I grow. Life asks that I be happy. Life asks that I procreate life. I need to answer YES, YES, YES! I say yes to life as I continue to study and learn the wonders of the universe. I say yes to life as I choose to see the good and the beautiful in everyone I meet and every situation I encounter. I say yes to life when I contribute a living act of love to the world.

♥ **AFFIRMATION** ♥

"With a smile, warm and genuine, on my lips, with unquestioning love in my heart, and with Spirit always on my mind, I say YES to life."

LOVE *is my only* MASTER

Today
I plant the seed of...

BEAUTIFYING MY HOME

Because Spirit is beauty, I am Divinely led to manifest the presence of this indwelling loveliness. I can reveal the splendor of Spirit in a myriad of ways but, in beautifying my home, I bring great joy to Heaven. Whether my home is great or small, in the heart of the Mother-Father God, it is consecrated as Sacred space by the presence of the Living Spirit of Divine Beauty.

♥   **AFFIRMATION**   ♥

**"From this day forward I dedicate my
home as a Holy temple, devoted only
to the nurturing of Spiritual Love and Beauty."**

LOVE *is my only* MASTER

---------------------------------- ♥ ----------------------------------

THY WILL

Sweet Spirit, so often I forget myself and allow my ego mind to lead me. I pray that you hold me near and guide me gently. I long to think the thoughts of Spirit and make manifest the dreams of Heaven. Help me then, Dear One to do Thy Will.

♥ **AFFIRMATION** ♥

"Thy Will is all that will be done in my life."

LOVE *is my only* MASTER

Today
I plant the seed of...

IGNORING GOSSIP

Idle words produced by idle minds create only suffering. The spreading of embellished half-truths is no less than verbal and emotional abuse. I must never allow my being to become poisoned by the likes of this brand of treachery.

♥ **AFFIRMATION** ♥

"Sweet Spirit, from my mouth, let there flow only words of kindness."

LOVE *is my only* MASTER

Today
I plant the seed of...

PSYCHIC SELF-PROTECTION

It is mandatory, before journeying out into the world each day, that I automatically surround and protect myself with the White Light of Love. Enveloped by this impenetrable cosmic force-field, I am shielded from every conceivable adversary of the Light.

♥   **AFFIRMATION**   ♥

"I am a Spiritual Warrior proudly donning the shield of the Everliving One."

LOVE *is my only* MASTER

Today
I plant the seed of…

CREATING MY REALITY

There is much talk being spread about concerning the upcoming "Great Shift". More than a shift of the earth on its axis, I must concern myself with a personal and planetary shift in consciousness. For through my personal consciousness, my personal reality is created. Private thoughts of peace and love create a more peaceful, loving world.

♥ **AFFIRMATION** ♥

"The state of my life reflects my state of mind."

LOVE *is my only* MASTER

Today
I plant the seed of...

FINANCIAL STABILITY

In the world of Spirit, truth will set my soul free. In the world of man, my physical freedom is attained through financial stability. It is my personal responsibility to see to it that I have sufficient finances to support my physical survival, my spiritual questing and my loftiest of dreams. Souls who have no money for food, have little time to ponder the wonders of Spirit.

♥　　　**AFFIRMATION**　　　♥

"Divine Oneness, as I free my mind from the struggle of finances, I free my hands and my heart to do Thy work."

LOVE *is my only* MASTER

Today
I plant the seed of...

EXPECT THE UNEXPECTED

Upon entering the physical realm, my soul understood that the life before me was designed to prepare me for Mastership. This journey can take as long as I like. My key to success is learning to ready myself, in all ways and at all times, for the unexpected. Attempting to second guess the Universe will only serve to assure my frustration.

♥ **AFFIRMATION** ♥

"By expecting the unexpected, I surrender my soul to the Infinite Wisdom of Spirit."

LOVE *is my only* MASTER

Today
I plant the seed of...

CLARITY

Through deep breathing and meditation I will purify my mind of all unwanted, outdated thought so that I may focus on my immediate circumstances with clear vision.

❤ **AFFIRMATION** ❤

**"My light becomes more
radiant as clarity fills my mind."**

LOVE *is my only* MASTER

♥

PURE INTENT

Once my mind is clear, I can examine my
personal motivations honestly. As a Child
of Light, I need to contribute to my global
family's well being. I need to be conscious
of how my heart thoughts touch the lives
of others.

♥   **AFFIRMATION**   ♥

**"I will infuse this day with my purest
intentions for the Highest Good of all."**

LOVE *is my only* MASTER

---------------- ♥ ----------------

PRIORITY

Life is an endless cycle of reaching and
attaining. After achieving clarity of
mind thru meditation and reflection, I
am guided to prioritize my goals. By so
doing, I cease to squander my time and
energy.

♥   AFFIRMATION   ♥

**"Today I turn my attention to understanding
what is important and what is more important."**

LOVE *is my only* MASTER

Today
I plant the seed of…

ACTION

With focused effort in a defined direction I will accomplish great things. As I isolate the important tasks to be accomplished this day, I waste no time moving towards that end.

♥ **AFFIRMATION** ♥

"Today I will initiate positive action in the direction of my desired success."

LOVE *is my only* MASTER

34

❤ ───────

FAITH

Knowing that manifestation is not often immediate, I put my faith into practice where tangible results seem to be lacking.

❤ **AFFIRMATION** ❤

**"My will is my wand, therefore,
I have faith that all my goals will be reached."**

LOVE *is my only* MASTER

35

Today
I plant the seed of...

PATIENCE

Spirit's perception of time and space differs vastly from my own. As a child of Spirit I need to respect the Infinite Wisdom of the All That Is and strive to develop the quality of patience.

♥ **AFFIRMATION** ♥

**"Every desire of my heart will come
to me in the perfect timing of Divine Spirit."**

LOVE *is my only* MASTER

Today
I plant the seed of...

RELAXATION

In order to truly appreciate the rewards of work welll done, I must learn to relax and enjoy leisure time. Whether I am reading, exercising, or planting daisies, allowing myself to unwind through pleasurable activity brings to me the jubilant nature of Spirit.

♥ **AFFIRMATION** ♥

"Today my goal is joy."

LOVE *is my only* MASTER

♥

Today
I plant the seed of...

BODY APPRECIATION

As I stand unclothed before a full length mirror, I admire my physical body. I now give bountiful thanks to my body for the countless ways it faithfully performs, on my behalf, each and every day.

♥   **AFFIRMATION**   ♥

"I fill my body with love and gratitude."

LOVE *is my only* MASTER

Today
I plant the seed of...

COMMUNICATING MY LOVE

Following my sacred path means that I allow myself to be Spirit led in all that I do. Today, Spirit leads me to fill my being with love. Therefore, it leads me to communicate the Holy Goddess' unconditional love through frequent acts of unselfishness and caring.

♥   **AFFIRMATION**   ♥

**"A heart full of love is an instrument
of the Holy Mother only when it
is emptied into the lives of others."**

LOVE *is my only* MASTER

Today
I plant the seed of...

SALUTING THE DIVINITY IN ALL

There is nothing in the Universe that brings more pain to the heart of God than the killing of her children in the name of religion. How can it be that we believe god to be love, yet we spread such hatred and horror in his name. I now avow to do all that I can to spread the love and kindness of a gentle God. I will begin by taking time to salute the Divinity in everyone I meet.

♥ **AFFIRMATION** ♥

"Holy Spirit, I honor you by saluting your Divine Presence in the heart of everyone I meet."

LOVE *is my only* MASTER

♥

Today
I plant the seed of...

BALANCE

While on the Earth plane, wholeness is my quest. Striving to maintain a working balance with my body, mind and spirit assures me of victory.

♥ **AFFIRMATION** ♥

"My life attracts only harmony."

LOVE *is my only* MASTER

Today
I plant the seed of…

RIGHTEOUS INDIGNATION

The world has been forever changed by the invention of the television, the computer and the magic of Hollywood. We have become so saturated with violence, atrocities and horror shows, that little seems to shock us anymore. As a Child of Light, I cannot allow this mental numbing to overtake me. I must take a stand, in righteous indignation, against anything that is harmful to the human spirit.

❤ **AFFIRMATION** ❤

"I am a torchbearer for the Light of Righteousness."

LOVE *is my only* MASTER

---❤---

VOLUNTEERING TIME TO MY COMMUNITY

There is no mistake that I find myself a member of my community. Life has placed me where I need to be so that I might teach and learn through community interaction. When there is nothing more to give or receive, where I am, life will move me elsewhere. In the meantime, I will help myself by helping others in my community.

❤ **AFFIRMATION** ❤

"A God-given talent becomes a gift of the greatest value when it is shared with others."

LOVE *is my only* MASTER

43

Today
I plant the seed of...

DESIGNING MY PRIVATE SANCTUARY

During times of contemplation and meditation, my experience of peace and serenity will be magnified if I place myself in a sanctuary of my own making. Into space I can bring my favorite spiritual objects, as well as, soothing smells, sounds and colors that further enhance the mood of Divinity I wish to create.

♥   **AFFIRMATION**   ♥

"I will design a private sanctuary which will recreate the beauteous serenity of my Indwelling Spirit."

LOVE *is my only* MASTER

♥

Today
I plant the seed of...

A RESPLENDENT PRESENCE

Each day I display the luminance of the Light of Spirit within me by means of my physical appearance. As a Child of Light, it is my duty to look and smell beautiful. The colors I choose, as well as the condition of the clothing I wear all reflect my state of Spirit.

♥ **AFFIRMATION** ♥

"My physical appearance brings light and beauty to the world."

LOVE *is my only* MASTER

♥

Today
I plant the seed of...

INTUITION

Many of my sensations and perceptions cannot be explained by logical means. I must learn to trust my spiritual insight and to depend upon my spontaneous knowing.

♥ **AFFIRMATION** ♥

"I will faithfully obey the small voice within me."

LOVE *is my only* MASTER

Today
I plant the seed of…

BROTHERHOOD

There is not a man, woman or child alive on Mother Earth this day who is not a precious member of my global family.

♥ **AFFIRMATION** ♥

**"I will recognize everyone
I meet as a Divine part of myself."**

LOVE *is my only* MASTER

Today
I plant the seed of...

ACCEPTANCE

I cannot always control the circumstances of my life. Nor am I always equipped to do so. Tranquility is mine for I know there is a Higher Intelligence at work in all my affairs.

♥ **AFFIRMATION** ♥

"In all ways, I will the Will of Spirit."

LOVE *is my only* MASTER

———————— ♥ ————————

LOVING KINDNESS

Offering a cheery hello to a stranger or extending a helpful hand to a soul in need are acts of kindness which I must train myself to perform automatically.

♥ **AFFIRMATION** ♥

**"I am the heart of Spirit
beating to the rhythm of love."**

LOVE *is my only* MASTER

49

Today
I plant the seed of…

NON-JUDGEMENT

On the road to enlightenment, there are many beyond me. Many more are dragging their feet behind me. It is my personal progress that needs to occupy my thoughts.

❤　**AFFIRMATION**　❤

"Starting with myself, I will view every soul as a reflection of perfection."

LOVE *is my only* MASTER

♥

Today
I plant the seed of...

HONORING MASCULINE ENERGY

Around the globe there are countless monuments honoring the genius and bravery of manhood. Of all the special tasks to be mastered through masculine energy, it is fatherhood that remains the most important and revered.

♥ **AFFIRMATION** ♥

"I salute and give thanks to the contributions of the Universal Masculine Force."

LOVE *is my only* MASTER

51

❤

Today
I plant the seed of…

IDEALISM

Race consciousness is limiting. I will now allow my higher mind to do my thinking. I will allow myself to be infused with light. I will draw inspiration from the bosom of Spirit.

❤ **AFFIRMATION** ❤

"I am propelled into genius by the Mind of Spirit."

LOVE *is my only* MASTER

♥

Today
I plant the seed of...

FLEXIBILITY

The one constant in physical life is change. Learning to be open to the unlimited variety of life's creative expression helps me to become a more fully integrated being.

♥ **AFFIRMATION** ♥

"I will gleefully dance to Spirit's changing melodies."

LOVE *is my only* MASTER

53

♥

Today
I plant the seed of…

CHARITY

To support a cause or individual that has no attachment to my personal way of being in the world, expands my identification with the Divine Oneness of All.

♥ **AFFIRMATION** ♥

"My acts of charity strengthen the presence of Spirit on Earth."

LOVE *is my only* MASTER

♥

Today
I plant the seed of...

RELATIONSHIPS

Each of us enters the garden alone.
Yet, without the gift of companionship,
through family and friends, life's music
falls on deaf ears.

♥   **AFFIRMATION**   ♥

**"I will consciously nurture all of
my relationships with tenderness."**

LOVE *is my only* MASTER

Today
I plant the seed of...

EMPOWERMENT

It is my responsibility in life to be my own most passionate advocate. I must defend myself from negativity and promote the flourishment of beauty in my sacred spaces.

♥ **AFFIRMATION** ♥

"I am empowered by the Great I Am."

LOVE *is my only* MASTER

♥

Today
I plant the seed of…

FORGIVENESS

The memory of all words and deeds that have harmed me I now release and cast upon the loving sea of spiritual understanding.

♥   **AFFIRMATION**   ♥

"I open my heart to hold only memories of love."

LOVE *is my only* MASTER

---------------------------- ♥ ----------------------------

Today
I plant the seed of…

ENTHUSIASM

As life springs eternally new I consciously ignite the spark of enthusiasm within. My life is to be a zestful testament to Spirit's exhilarating vibration.

♥   **AFFIRMATION**   ♥

**"I create each new day,
with enthusiasm and excitement."**

LOVE *is my only* MASTER

--- ♥ ---

DETACHED COMPASSION

Detached compassion is learning to care for the sick without coming down with the disease. I cannot allow the sorrows and disappointments of others to place obstacles upon my path.

♥ **AFFIRMATION** ♥

**"I am not a beast of burden to carry others.
Instead, I aspire to be a torch to light their way."**

LOVE *is my only* MASTER

♥

Today
I plant the seed of…

SELF-LOVE

Without vanity or conceit I am happy to be me. I am proud of who I am becoming and the spiritual lessons I have mastered.

♥ **AFFIRMATION** ♥

"I am love."

LOVE *is my only* MASTER

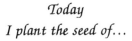

Today
I plant the seed of...

CELEBRATION

Life is the most extraordinary collage of splendiferous events. Witnessing a sunrise, listening to the call of a mother robin or bathing myself in pale moonlight are all activities that beseech me to join the celebration of life.

♥ AFFIRMATION ♥

"I celebrate life and find joy in every experience."

LOVE *is my only* MASTER

♥

SILENCE

True strength and wisdom are found in being completely still. My words can often cloud my spiritual vision. In my haste to answer life's call I can confuse what I am being asked.

♥ **AFFIRMATION** ♥

"By honoring the sacredness of silence, I hold my words until Spirit moves me to speak its truth."

LOVE *is my only* MASTER

REPROGRAMMING

So much of what I do and say are leftovers from the child or young adult I used to be. Today I am much wiser and more in touch with myself, therefore, I choose to reprogram myself from this new perspective I have on life.

♥ **AFFIRMATION** ♥

"I live only in the now, and my reactions are based on this moment only."

LOVE *is my only* MASTER

Today
I plant the seed of…

NATIONAL PRIDE

I realize the many freedoms that bless my life in this country. No nation on this globe has reached political perfection. I stand proud to be a member of this great country and I will help her, however I can, to heal her wounds.

♥ **AFFIRMATION** ♥

"For all the positive energy my country has generated on behalf of this world, I am proud of her."

LOVE *is my only* MASTER

64

♥

New Experiences

There are infinite opportunities awaiting me to experience something totally novel. I could learn to skate, take voice lessons or plan a trip around the world. Wherever my interests lie, life is inviting me to live.

♥ **Affirmation** ♥

"I am open and willing to live life in a fresh and courageous manner."

LOVE *is my only* MASTER

♥

CHOICE

As I entered this physical realm, I brought with me two things: my personal mission and free will. I am free to choose happiness, enlightenment and higher thought, no matter what circumstances challenge me this day.

♥   **AFFIRMATION**   ♥

"I protect and encourage my right to choose the best in myself, for myself, always."

LOVE *is my only* MASTER

---------- ♥ ----------

Today
I plant the seed of...

THANKSGIVING

I am eternally grateful for the love that laces my life with joy. I am beholden to the friends and family that offer me acceptance and I am obliged to the situations that urge me to grow.

♥   **AFFIRMATION**   ♥

**"I am thankful to Great Spirit for
the showering of life's treasures, great and small."**

LOVE *is my only* MASTER

67

Today
I plant the seed of...

DEMONSTRATION

There is a need in this world for a show of love and light. In my personal world, I vow to demonstrate the love of Spirit in very obvious and tangible ways.

❤ **AFFIRMATION** ❤

**"I will express my love and
spread my light to all I encounter."**

LOVE *is my only* MASTER

Today
I plant the seed of…

STUDIOUSNESS

At this point in our earth's history, many light beings are channeling the wisdom of the Elevated Ones. There is much for me to rediscover about myself and through studying the works of these channels of light, I will be edified.

♥ **AFFIRMATION** ♥

"The more I study and meditate upon words of light, the more luminous I become."

LOVE *is my only* MASTER

--- ❤ ---

DISCERNMENT

It has been said that truth will light upon my heart like the wings of an angel. So, it is feasible that I might overlook this gentle sign. Discernment is a quality of Spirit, when developed, that allows me to know when truth is spoken.

❤ **AFFIRMATION** ❤

"I ask Spirit to bless me with the gift of discernment."

LOVE *is my only* MASTER

―――――――――――――― ♥ ――――――――――――――

COMPANIONSHIP

So often I tell friends that we must get together, yet I do nothing to make that invitation a reality. Today I will reach out to a friend and bring cheer into both our lives.

♥ **AFFIRMATION** ♥

"In the company of friends I will find the laughter and Joy of Spirit. "

LOVE *is my only* MASTER

♥

ARTISTRY

Each soul is an instrument of Spirit's creativity. Within me there lies talent and artistry in the area of my choosing. Whether I am a writer or mother, painter or mason, I express myself with artistry.

♥ ## AFFIRMATION ♥

"My personal artistry brings color and imagination to my every task."

LOVE *is my only* MASTER

Today
I plant the seed of...

LEADERSHIP

Since I am a seeker of light, wherever I find myself, I am in a position to lead those near me to the light as well. As a spiritual being I can offer myself and my life as an example leading as I have been led.

❤ ## AFFIRMATION ❤

**"Through my example I can lead
others to the Light of Spirit."**

LOVE *is my only* MASTER

Today
I plant the seed of...

PRAISE

Each of us on Earth, during these tumultuous times, is doing our best. All too often I forget to let my brothers and sisters know how much I appreciate their efforts to bring their uniqueness to our world.

♥ **AFFIRMATION** ♥

**"I will lift my voice in praise
for every kindred soul in Spirit."**

LOVE *is my only* MASTER

---------------------------- ♥ ----------------------------

ABUNDANCE

In the eyes of creative Spirit there is only abundance. Everything put upon this living planet was placed here lavishly. Abundance is my personal birthright.

♥   **AFFIRMATION**   ♥

**"It is the Will of Heaven, so I now open
my heart to receive lavish abundance in all things."**

LOVE *is my only* MASTER

♥

Today
I plant the seed of...

THOUGHTFULNESS

A note sent to cheer a loved one, a flower purchased to say I love you or a dinner invitation for no special reason are just a few of the things I can do to show those dear to me that I think of them with love.

♥ ## AFFIRMATION ♥

**"Great Spirit, lead my heart to
do your works through thoughtfulness."**

LOVE *is my only* MASTER

♥ ────────

Today
I plant the seed of...

GENTLE STRENGTH

The way of the TAO is the art of gentleness. As a Spiritual Warrior, I show my greatest strength when my sword is made of gentle words and loving actions.

♥ **AFFIRMATION** ♥

"In all ways, let me penetrate the veil of ignorance with gentleness."

LOVE *is my only* MASTER

Today
I plant the seed of…

SPIRITUAL FLUENCY

Not everyone I meet recognizes the same spiritual alphabet. Our languages may differ, but our Source is the same. I must learn to be a spiritual linguist, speaking and hearing words that bring me ever closer to my human family.

♥　　　**AFFIRMATION**　　　♥

"I will speak from an open heart and I will allow Spirit to be my loving interpreter."

LOVE *is my only* MASTER

Today
I plant the seed of...

DAYDREAMING

There is nothing that has ever been accomplished that I cannot accomplish...and more. Learning to daydream again can strengthen my spirit, uplift my heart and empower my daily efforts.

♥ **AFFIRMATION** ♥

**"The fulfillment of all my dreams
is part of Spirit's Divine plan."**

LOVE *is my only* MASTER

79

———————— ❤ ————————

Today
I plant the seed of...

COMMUNION

As the pressures of the realm draw near to my sacred space, I discipline myself to automatically initiate communion with my highest self. In this practice, my spiritual balance need never be endangered.

❤ **AFFIRMATION** ❤

"I encircle myself with the Violet Ray, as I spiritually commune with my purest inbeing."

LOVE *is my only* MASTER

80

Today
I plant the seed of...

EVOLUTION

I have studied, meditated and
affirmed my way to a certain level
of spiritual confidence. Yet the
truth I seek is as eternal and
dynamic as my Loving Source.

♥　　**AFFIRMATION**　　♥

"I am poised, ready to receive any and all new
information which will facilitate my soul's evolution."

LOVE *is my only* MASTER

81

Today
I plant the seed of…

REINFORCING MY GOOD

The inequities of this realm are bois-
terously broadcast from dawn to
moonrise. To achieve my spiritual
ends, I must constantly remind
myself of all that is right and perfect
in my world.

♥   **AFFIRMATION**   ♥

"As a spiritual being, my reality is love and light."

LOVE *is my only* MASTER

Today
I plant the seed of...

MY CHRISTHOOD

Within my soul there dwells the power and majesty of Infinite Spirit. I now call forth the purity of the Christed One within me to be born anew. In reference to the Mother-Father-god, with sacred longing in my heart, I declare my Christhood. I Am the Way, the Truth and the Life.

♥ **AFFIRMATION** ♥

"My ascension into the realm of Light commences the instant I proclaim my Christhood."

LOVE *is my only* MASTER

❤

JUBILATION

As I begin this new day I will visualize myself experiencing only joy and happiness. I will see myself breathing cheer and jubilation into everyone and everything I touch.

❤ **AFFIRMATION** ❤

**"My life is a jubilant expression
of my Creator's perfection."**

LOVE *is my only* MASTER

84

Today
I plant the seed of...

SELFLESSNESS

As an emissary of the Great Spirit, I have come to Mother Earth to serve her and her children through my unique contribution. Teach me, Great One, to become selfless in my giving and steadfast in my efforts.

♥ **AFFIRMATION** ♥

"As I give of myself without thought of reward, I am rewarded beyond measure."

LOVE *is my only* MASTER

85

♥

Today
I plant the seed of...

UNIVERSAL RHYTHM

There is a natural rhythm to the universe, an underlying, ever so subtle, musical theme to which life within dances. Once I attune myself to the rhythm of the cosmos, my life will flow to the beat of perfection.

♥   **AFFIRMATION**   ♥

"I will choreograph my life to the music of the Celestial Composer."

LOVE *is my only* MASTER

Today
I plant the seed of...

SINGLE VISION

When my energies are scattered it is
difficult for me to influence my world
with real power. As I narrow my vision
and streamline my field of purpose, I
am more likely to impact others and
accomplish great things.

♥ **AFFIRMATION** ♥

**"As I train my eyes to have single
vision, my true abilities come into focus."**

LOVE *is my only* MASTER

♥

Today
I plant the seed of...

THE PURGING OF DARKNESS

As the Earth approaches the end of this century, humankind is being purged of its' ignorance and insanity. Darkness may appear to prevail for a time, but, I will take heart in the bleakest of times, knowing that Spirit is cleansing the human psyche in preparation for the dawning of the Aquarian Age of Peace.

♥ **AFFIRMATION** ♥

**"I will rise above the appearance
of tragedy and darkest disaster by
holding firmly to Holy Spirit's Wings of Love."**

LOVE *is my only* MASTER

---------- ♥ ----------

SPIRITUAL MATURITY

No longer am I a babe in the Universe. I have been here, in one fashion or another since time immemorium. I now am cognizant of my responsibility to my Universal family and I vow to spread the Light of Spirit wherever I may travel.

♥ **AFFIRMATION** ♥

"As the human condition appears to be regressing, Mother Earth requests my spiritual maturity."

LOVE *is my only* MASTER

Today
I plant the seed of...

STAMINA

The workload of the spiritual warrior is exhausting. There are few thanks and long hours. Yet the battle for enlightenment cannot be abandoned. I play a vital role in the salvation of my brotherhood.

❤ **AFFIRMATION** ❤

**"Give me stamina, Dear One,
and lead me to Thy victory."**

LOVE *is my only* MASTER

Today
I plant the seed of...

SINGING SPIRIT'S PRAISES

Like a wilted flower, I can be rejuvenated by the loving words of encouragement and praise of a kindred spirit. In the same way, the Infinite Energy of the Great Spirit is magnified by my words of loving praise.

❤ **AFFIRMATION** ❤

"In all things, let me praise the Magnificence of Spirit."

LOVE *is my only* MASTER

Today
I plant the seed of…

RELINQUISHING MY BELIEF IN DUALITY

If I so choose, I have the free will to concentrate my attention on that which is troubling, dark and hateful in life. Or, I can choose to keep my mind focused on all things beautiful and loving. Belief in duality is learned behavior. It is a conditioned response to physical life. Duality does not exist in the Mind of God, therefore, it does not exist.

♥ **AFFIRMATION** ♥

"In all that I embrace in life, there is only good, for God is Good, and Good is All That Is."

LOVE *is my only* MASTER

♥

Today
I plant the seed of...

INDIVIDUAL OPINION

The One Light of Christ Consciousness manifests as millions of seemingly individual shining rays. Yet, each singular beam of light is but a reflection of the Original Source. For those traveling the lighted path, the opinions of others are to be regarded as respectfully as personal reflections of Universal Truth.

♥ **AFFIRMATION** ♥

**"I will respect the individual opinions of
my Earthly companions for I understand
the One Light is reflected in a multitude of ways."**

LOVE *is my only* MASTER

Today
I plant the seed of...

HONORING HARD WORK

To labor in the name of Spirit is indeed
an honor in and of itself. It may appear
that I work for money, yet in truth, I toil
for the love of heaven. Whatever task
busies my hands and mind each day, is
truly part of my Divine mission.

♥ **AFFIRMATION** ♥

**"Until the pure Light of Heaven shines
in the hearts of all humankind, I am
dedicated to hard work on Spirit's behalf."**

LOVE *is my only* MASTER

Today
I plant the seed of...

ORGANIZATION

In the Infinite Mind of Spirit, there is a place for everything and everything is in its place. In my personal life I seek to emulate this Divine order. Organizing my home, my time and thoughts increase my spiritual authenticity as I release myself from the enervation of clutter.

♥   **AFFIRMATION**   ♥

"Infinite Mind, please bless my efforts to express Divine order in my daily life."

LOVE *is my only* MASTER

95

Today
I plant the seed of…

PRODUCTIVITY

It is not enough that I go through the motions of my life. Today I long to feel truly productive. To be productive does not mean that I must do more. It means that I must strive to be more and to share more of myself, for the upliftment of others.

♥ **AFFIRMATION** ♥

"Holy Spirit, I ask to be your unfettered vessel so that I may produce the kind of spiritual results that make life, on Earth more meaningful."

LOVE *is my only* MASTER

Today
I plant the seed of...

PAYING ATTENTION TO DETAIL

The Cosmic Powers are constantly feeding me vital information from every direction. Yet, I often miss these important messages because I am not paying attention to detail. In my ignorance, I've dismissed the words of strangers, chalked up destiny to coincidence and worse yet, I tend to overlook the obvious.

♥ **AFFIRMATION** ♥

"I witness the presence of Spirit in every aspect of life when I learn to pay attention to detail."

LOVE *is my only* MASTER

♥

BODY LANGUAGE

The way I hold my head, use my eyes and carry my body all affect my personal vibration and the way I feel within my being.

♥   **AFFIRMATION**   ♥

"In all circumstances, out of self-love, I project my Divine Nature."

LOVE *is my only* MASTER

♥

─────────────────────── ♥ ───────────────────────

Today
I plant the seed of...

CONTACTING MY HIGHEST SELF

I am a multidimensional being. Simultaneously, I exist on all levels of consciousness. My Higher Self, that eternal part of me closest to the Holy Spirit, is always just a breath away. I can call on my Higher Self at any time for the wisdom and love I need.

♥ **AFFIRMATION** ♥

"My Highest Self stands ready to lift me up in consciousness whenever I am ready to ask."

LOVE *is my only* MASTER

Today
I plant the seed of...

TREASURING CHILDREN

Every child I meet is a reflection of the vibrant energy, purity and boundless love emanating from the Original Source. Children are most blessed. They are the closest thing to perfection on earth. To treasure and protect the children is a divine act of spiritual understanding.

♥ **AFFIRMATION** ♥

"Holy One, please bless me with a heart that reaches out in love to all children."

LOVE *is my only* MASTER

Today
I plant the seed of...

SPIRIT IN FORM

To understand my eternal identity is to understand that I am Spirit in form. Spirit is the power that animates my life. The breath of my being is the life force of Spirit. To grasp this fact is to unveil a great mystery.

♥ **AFFIRMATION** ♥

"While expressing myself as a physical being, I am manifesting as Spirit in form."

LOVE *is my only* MASTER

♥

SELF-REALIZATION

As a spiritual being inhabiting a physical body, I sometimes forget my eternal reality. In truth, I am one with Spirit. I am boundless love. I am endless light.

♥   **AFFIRMATION**   ♥

"I must constantly remind myself of my spiritual identify for self-realization is my key to Peace on Earth."

LOVE *is my only* MASTER

102

---------- ♥ ----------

ASSIMILATION

All month I have worked to achieve something of substance. Today I will retreat from the activity of the outer world and assimilate all of the thoughts and words that I have previously absorbed as energy.

♥   **AFFIRMATION**   ♥

"A routine assimilation of internal energy promotes my personal clarity and well-being."

LOVE *is my only* MASTER

Today
I plant the seed of...

CHEERFUL SEPARATION

In every life there comes a time when two souls who have shared so much, come to a fork in their road. This may be so for lovers, business partners, good friends or family members. No matter who is involved, separating paths can be quite painful to endure. Yet, in Spirit, two that have come together in the presence of love, shall be connected forevermore.

♥ **AFFIRMATION** ♥

"By co-operating with a cheerful separation, I free us both to honor our sacred pathways."

LOVE *is my only* MASTER

❤

Today
I plant the seed of...

HARMONIZING MY ENVIRONMENT

The spaces in which I spend the majority
of my time will actually contribute to my
physical and spiritual well-being if their
energy harmonizes with my own. Proper
lighting and color combine to elevate
my mood and quicken my spirit.

❤   ## AFFIRMATION   ❤

**"For love of self, I need to harmonize my
environment with the vibration of my true essence."**

LOVE *is my only* MASTER

105

Today
I plant the seed of...

KNOWINGNESS

I cannot rely on the appearance of the present as a means of predicting the future. When I know in my heart, unwaveringly, where I want to go and what I want to achieve, there are no challenges that can stop me.

❤ **AFFIRMATION** ❤

"My knowingness tells me that my dreams were first dreamed, for me, by Spirit."

LOVE *is my only* MASTER

♥

Today
I plant the seed of...

SURRENDER

So often I wrangle with Spirit over the terms of life in the physical realm. I want the human condition to conform to my internal picture, instead of accepting its present level of evolution. I recurrently find myself resisting the natural rhythms of the Earth Dance.

♥ **AFFIRMATION** ♥

"I must sagaciously surrender to life by allowing Spirit to set the tempo and take the lead."

LOVE *is my only* MASTER

107

♥

Today
I plant the seed of...

GOOD HUMOR

On the bleakest occasions, a light touch and a contagious giggle can work true magic. In the darkest of times, my indwelling spirit can dance with glee to the sound of merriment.

♥ **AFFIRMATION** ♥

**"I cast the bright light of hope
when I call upon the Spirit of humor."**

LOVE *is my only* MASTER

108

─────────── ❤ ───────────

EMOTIONAL MASTERY

As a spiritual warrior, it is paramount that I am master of my emotions. In order to carry out the intricate details of my earth assignment, I must have unyielding control over my thoughts, words and deeds.

❤   **AFFIRMATION**   ❤

**"I am master of my fate when
I am master of my emotions."**

LOVE *is my only* MASTER

♥

Today
I plant the seed of...

KEEPING A JOURNAL

My personal journey towards wholeness
has taken me down many backroads
and up just as many mountain trails. By
recording daily entries into a spiritual
journal, I intensify my cognitive process
and accelerate my spiritual evolution.

♥   **AFFIRMATION**   ♥

**"A personal journal helps to keep me on
course as I tread the path to At-One-Ment."**

LOVE *is my only* MASTER

---❤---

Today
I plant the seed of...

THE POWER OF PEACE

When I sustain only thoughts of love, I open myself to the experience of peace beyond measure. My day may be decorated in an eclectic showcase of people and circumstances that either help to focus or distract me. Yet, my daily mission is to bring the peace of Spirit into every situation I encounter.

❤   **AFFIRMATION**   ❤

"Connecting my mind with the Divine Mind guarantees me the Power of Peace."

LOVE *is my only* MASTER

Today
I plant the seed of...

QUALITY

The living of my life is like the crafting of an exquisite piece of jewelry. First I must decide if I want the foundation of my life to be laid in gold or silver. Then I must carefully choose the gems that will reflect my luminance. The quality of my materials and the degree of my craftsmanship will determine, long after I am gone, whether or not this lifetime held true value.

❤ **AFFIRMATION** ❤

"Crafting a quality life is my gift to Spirit."

LOVE *is my only* MASTER

Today
I plant the seed of...

TRUST

As the Earth is preparing for the coming of the New Age of Peace, there are many happenings and events taking place which leave me confused and unsettled. Yet, I know that I am to remain firmly anchored to my spiritual beliefs in Omnipotence of the Divine Plan now unfolding.

♥   **AFFIRMATION**   ♥

"I trust my soul to see the Light of Spirit where my physical eyes can see naught."

LOVE *is my only* MASTER

♥

Today
I plant the seed of...

VIGILANCE

So often I am tempted to allow my humanness the first response to life. Living from within the Light of Spirit, more often requires more concentrated effort on my part.

♥ **AFFIRMATION** ♥

"I am vigilant in my mission as a Torchbearer of Spirit's Living Light."

LOVE *is my only* MASTER

114

♥

LIVING IN THE NOW

By longing for days gone by or striving for times yet to come, I rob myself of the joy inherent in every present experience. Now is the only time I have to be happy. I must embrace each day as if it were the only one I will ever have.

♥ **AFFIRMATION** ♥

"Living in the now increases my ability to experience and share the Joy of Spirit."

LOVE *is my only* MASTER

♥

Today
I plant the seed of...

WHOLESOMENESS

To be a whole, self-actualized and a
contributing member of humanity, I
need to do all I can to increase my
spiritual frequency. I achieve this end
as I seek to emulate the wholesome
Nature of Spirit.

♥ **AFFIRMATION** ♥

**"May the Divine Mind fill my soul with the
innocence and purity of its wholesomeness."**

LOVE *is my only* MASTER

116

Today
I plant the seed of...

SPIRITUAL GIFTS

The Holy Spirit has blessed me with abundant gifts and talents. It is part of my earth assignment to recognize, strengthen and utilize these gifts to my highest potential, for the good of all.

♥ **AFFIRMATION** ♥

"I devote the use of my divinely given gifts and talents to the upliftment of humankind."

LOVE *is my only* MASTER

Today
I plant the seed of...

DIVINE RECOGNITION

As I behold the Light of Spirit shining forth from within my being, I need to recognize that light as existing within each and every soul who happens across my path.

♥ **AFFIRMATION** ♥

"I recognize the Divine Light of love within each soul who touches my life."

LOVE *is my only* MASTER

---❤---

SOOTHING SOUND

There is a cosmic sound, a celestial choir forever chanting a placid accompaniment to the pulse of my personal energy.

❤   **AFFIRMATION**   ❤

"With Spirit in my heart, I will compose a symphony of personal tranquility."

LOVE *is my only* MASTER

119

♥

Today
I plant the seed of...

COMMITMENT

In order to successfully fulfill my soul's purpose, I need to be committed to calling forth the best and brightest from within myself.

♥ **AFFIRMATION** ♥

"I now commit my soul to the fulfillment of every spiritual ideal."

LOVE *is my only* MASTER

♥

Today
I plant the seed of...

ACTIVE LISTENING

I nurture myself as I nurture my Earth family. When I am actively listening to the feelings and thoughts of those I know and love, I am nurturing a Divine aspect within both of us.

♥ **AFFIRMATION** ♥

"By listening to the heart of humankind, I will surely hear the Voice of Spirit."

LOVE *is my only* MASTER

Today
I plant the seed of...

CERTAINTY

All about me there are tragedies occurring in the lives of my global family. Even so, frustration and doubt cannot be granted admittance into my personal realm.

♥ **AFFIRMATION** ♥

"With unshakable certainty, I place my life in the hands of Infinite Wisdom."

LOVE *is my only* MASTER

--- ♥ ---

Today
I plant the seed of...

ROMANCE

My relationship to my Divine Source is romantic on the most grand scale. Spirit and I are one and the same. We are inseparable and bound eternally by love.

♥ **AFFIRMATION** ♥

**"I am made whole by giving
and receiving the Love of Spirit."**

LOVE *is my only* MASTER

---❤---

Today
I plant the seed of...

SIMPLICITY

I can be truest to my spiritual path
when I simplify my life and keep my
eye single. Focusing on one task at
a time allows me to keep myself in
perfect balance.

❤ **AFFIRMATION** ❤

"As I simplify my life I magnify my personal power."

LOVE *is my only* MASTER

———————— ♥ ————————

WEALTH

Sharing precious moments with the ones I love, enjoying glowing health and recognizing the Universal Consciousness within me are all 24 karat blessings in my life.

♥   **AFFIRMATION**   ♥

**"Through the Gifts of Spirit,
I find true and lasting wealth."**

LOVE *is my only* MASTER

125

❤

Today
I plant the seed of...

PARTNERSHIP

Many spiritual seekers have felt that, according to Cosmic Will, their lives simply unfold as necessary. Yet, I have learned that Spirit and I are co-creators of my life.

❤ **AFFIRMATION** ❤

"In partnership, Spirit and I collaborate to create within my life something we both can be proud of."

LOVE *is my only* MASTER

126

❤

OBEDIENCE

As I endeavor to attune myself to the frequency of Spirit, it is not enough to simply pride myself on hearing the small voice within. It is my duty to also obey.

❤ **AFFIRMATION** ❤

"My intuition is meaningless without demonstrating obedience to the Spirit who guides me."

LOVE *is my only* MASTER

--- ♥ ---

TIMING

In life, achievements and blessings are a matter of timing. After I have affirmed my desire and projected my gratitude and positivism into the Cosmos, I then need to rely on the perfection of Spirit's timing.

♥ **AFFIRMATION** ♥

**"In the right and perfect time,
all my dreams shall be fulfilled."**

LOVE *is my only* MASTER

Today
I plant the seed of...

DIVINE OBSTACLES

From time to time I attract restrictions and limitations that cause me to feel that my spiritual progress is being hampered. In reality, every difficulty serves my highest good.

♥ **AFFIRMATION** ♥

**"I behold a loving blessing in each
Divine obstacle I have chosen to experience."**

LOVE *is my only* MASTER

---- ♥ ----

EVALUATION

At varying intervals in my life, it is benefi-
cial for me to take stock of what I have
absorbed and assimilated from my myriad
of life occurrences.

♥   AFFIRMATION   ♥

**"By evaluating my present status, I
act to reset my course and empower my future."**

LOVE *is my only* MASTER

---❤---

HAPPINESS

Spirit desires that I know only happiness.
The attainment of true happiness is my
destiny.

❤ **AFFIRMATION** ❤

**"My happiness lies where my will
and the Will of Heaven meet as one."**

LOVE *is my only* MASTER

131

Today
I plant the seed of...

HOPE

All of the peace and harmony that I
long to see made manifest on Earth is
now being created from the very fabric
of my desires.

♥ **AFFIRMATION** ♥

**"Dear Spirit, from my heart,
let there shine a ray of Eternal Hope."**

LOVE *is my only* MASTER

Today
I plant the seed of…

MODERATION

As a Spiritual Warrior, I must achieve self-restraint. As I climb to higher spiritual heights, I experience a narrowing of my path. Traveling too far to the left or right may cause me to lose my Divine footing.

♥ **AFFIRMATION** ♥

**"Moderation is the path leading
to the Spiritual Warrior's victory."**

LOVE *is my only* MASTER

---♥---

WORSHIP

By honoring the Sacred Spirit within all living things, I worship my Creator. By cultivating the beauty of my inner and outer nature, I worship my Source.

♥ **AFFIRMATION** ♥

"To worship the Great Spirit is to remain conscious of its Omnipresence."

LOVE *is my only* MASTER

♥

RELIABILITY

Good intentions are not good enough. As a Child of Light, I have made a promise to the Universe to live in a manner which reflects my ability to be a reliable vessel for the Spirit of Truth.

♥ ### AFFIRMATION ♥

"My words and actions must mirror my spiritual reliability."

LOVE *is my only* MASTER

135

Today
I plant the seed of...

INDEPENDENCE

Although there is only one Spirit animating all life forms upon this planet, my mind, body and earth mission are highly unique and one of a kind. I cannot allow myself to be bound by the personal truth of anyone else.

♥ **AFFIRMATION** ♥

**"Living my personal vision
requires spiritual independence."**

LOVE *is my only* MASTER

♥

REINVENTION

My personality is the product of my experiences heretofore. I can chose at any time, to reinvent myself. If I want to be more robust or more calm, that is just a decision away.

♥   **AFFIRMATION**   ♥

"The privilege of reinventing myself is granted me by the Living Power of Spirit."

LOVE *is my only* MASTER

♥

Today
I plant the seed of...

PLAYFULNESS

It is only in the openness of the childlike Spirit that I will experience the pure joy of Heaven on Earth. To giggle, to be playful and innocent is my passport to spiritual bliss.

♥ **AFFIRMATION** ♥

"To exhibit playfulness is to feel Divine."

LOVE *is my only* MASTER

♥

CONSCIOUS BREATHING

The body I inhabit is nourished by food, water and air. Inhaling the cosmic breath of life deeply and consciously is as important as eating whole foods and drinking pure water.

♥ **AFFIRMATION** ♥

"Being conscious of my breathing keeps me conscious of the vital Life Force within me."

LOVE *is my only* MASTER

139

♥

INNER VISION

As I give attention to newspapers and television, I receive an unsettling picture of the outer world. Yet, through my inner vision, I can view the world more positively.

♥ **AFFIRMATION** ♥

"Divine Spirit creates only pictures of love and light for my inner vision."

LOVE *is my only* MASTER

Today
I plant the seed of...

WHOLENESS

It is my spiritual quest to unify all facets of my being into one loving and integrated whole. By removing from myself all thought of separateness from Spirit, I take giant leaps towards wholeness.

♥ ## AFFIRMATION ♥

"I am Spirit made manifest on Earth."

LOVE *is my only* MASTER

Today
I plant the seed of...

MEDITATION

Only in the eye of the hurricane can peace and quiet be found. Life in the outer world often resembles the chaos of a hurricane. The art of meditation removes me from the outer storm and offers me the true serenity residing within my soul.

❤ **AFFIRMATION** ❤

**"Through the art of meditation
I find my home in serenity."**

LOVE *is my only* MASTER

Today
I plant the seed of...

ILLUMINATION

In truth, I am a light being. Today I will sit quietly and envision my light body. It is brilliant and perfect. Once I visualize it, I will increase the brightness of my light body until it illuminates my physical body as well.

❤ **AFFIRMATION** ❤

"I am illuminated by the radiance of Divine Spirit."

LOVE *is my only* MASTER

Today
I plant the seed of…

ONENESS WITH NATURE

Sitting beside a large old tree or upon an ancient boulder is an excellent way to exchange energy and forge a lasting bond with the natural powers on Earth.

♥ **AFFIRMATION** ♥

"I am spiritually grounded by time spent in the splendor of nature."

LOVE *is my only* MASTER

Today
I plant the seed of...

PERFECT ALIGNMENT

The Universe is a place of Divine Order. I have traveled to Earth in order to perfect my ability to align my physical being with the spiritual perfection of the cosmos.

♥ **AFFIRMATION** ♥

"In light, Universal perfection is now and has always been my reality."

LOVE *is my only* MASTER

♥

PERSONAL EXPANSION

There are innumerable paths up the mountainside of enlightenment. My spiritual philosophy my be enhanced and expanded by study-ing the wisdoms sacred to other peoples and cultures.

♥ **AFFIRMATION** ♥

"I inspire my personal expansion by investigating other spiritual beliefs held dear by my global family."

LOVE *is my only* MASTER

146

Today
I plant the seed of...

VISION

As a Spiritual Warrior, I seek to view life as through the eyes of Spirit. As I succeed at this, an exhilarating panorama of love and purpose unfold before me.

♥   **AFFIRMATION**   ♥

**"When my spiritual eyes are focused,
I behold only visions of endless love."**

LOVE *is my only* MASTER

Today
I plant the seed of...

WISDOM

Through my studies and meditations, the words of the Masters flood my being. Yet, only when I courageously live in the light of truth do I attain genuine wisdom.

♥ **AFFIRMATION** ♥

"I am wise when the words of the Masters become my living testament."

LOVE *is my only* MASTER

Today
I plant the seed of...

QUIETUDE

As I calm my environment by controlling the external din, I enhance the growth of internal peace through quietude.

♥ **AFFIRMATION** ♥

"In quietude, I contact my truest essence."

LOVE *is my only* MASTER

Today
I plant the seed of…

LESSON LEARNING

I am consciously co-operating with
my spiritual evolution when I believe
that every circumstance in my life has
been attracted to introduce me to
yet another aspect of Infinite
Intelligence.

♥   **AFFIRMATION**   ♥

**"Dear Spirit, bless my awareness with the
Divine Intelligence creating my every experience."**

LOVE *is my only* MASTER

Today
I plant the seed of...

QUESTING

I liken my life to the quest of the
knights of old. I too search for the
Holy Grail, that sacred cup said to
hold the secret of eternal life. My
search, however, does not take me
far and away.

♥ **AFFIRMATION** ♥

**"My quest for eternal life begins and ends
with the discovery of my Indwelling Spirit."**

LOVE *is my only* MASTER

Today
I plant the seed of...

REJOICING

Every day that I spend on Earth is a festive occasion worthy of celebration. As I mature spiritually, my capacity for experiencing joy deepens.

♥ **AFFIRMATION** ♥

"As I rejoice in the living of my life, I glorify Spirit."

LOVE *is my only* MASTER

152

―――――――――――――――――― ♥ ――――――――――――――――――

LETTING GO

It is human nature for me to hang onto
the habits and hopes of yesterday. Yet,
my Divine Nature asks that I live totally
in the now while I prepare myself to
receive the gifts and blessings awaiting
me.

♥   **AFFIRMATION**   ♥

**"I continually manifest my Highest Good,
as I let goand let Divine Spirit flow through me."**

LOVE *is my only* MASTER

---❤---

THOUGHTFUL THINKING

How often I find myself contemplating thoughts representing less than the highest good for myself and others. As I remind myself that thoughts are things, I need to be more thoughtful of the things I am creating.

❤ **AFFIRMATION** ❤

"Infinite Spirit, please help me to consistently live in your loving thoughts."

LOVE *is my only* MASTER

─────────────── ♥ ───────────────

THE CHILD WITHIN

Infinite Mind manifests in me as limitless imagination. The child within is most gifted at the use of this imagination, weaving magical dreams of Heaven on Earth.

♥　　　**AFFIRMATION**　　　♥

"Through the child within I recapture the magic of my being."

LOVE *is my only* MASTER

155

Today
I plant the seed of...

FEELING GOOD

My mind has the power to influence my body and emotions. As I mentally resolve to live fully and enjoy all aspects of my day, I align myself more easily with positive Universal Energy.

❤   **AFFIRMATION**   ❤

"Feeling good in body and spirit is a matter of adopting a positive state of mind."

LOVE *is my only* MASTER

---❤---

POLITENESS

As an individuation of Spirit, I am a child of majesty. In remembering my royal inheritance, I must never forget my spiritual decorum. With a demeanor of courtliness, I must address each member of my Earth Family with politeness, no matter what the circumstance.

❤ ### AFFIRMATION ❤

"As an emissary of Spirit, I display only genuine politeness through my personal interchanges."

LOVE *is my only* MASTER

Today
I plant the seed of...

UNLEARNING

Of all the tasks before me on my path towards spiritual mastery, unlearning is the most challenging task of all. To unlearn the lessons of my youth, to unlearn the beliefs of my original family is indeed formidable.

♥ **AFFIRMATION** ♥

"With conscious effort I will position myself to unlearn any and all beliefs that do not support my present level of spiritual awareness."

LOVE *is my only* MASTER

---❤---

FEARLESSNESS

I am a Spiritual Warrior, pledged to the preservation of Universal Life. My Earth assignment demands that I be fearless in my personal propagation of peace and unconditional love.

❤   **AFFIRMATION**   ❤

"There is no greater power than love, and I will be fearless as I live my life in service to love's power."

LOVE *is my only* MASTER

159

Today
I plant the seed of...

WONDER

Everywhere I travel upon this sacred sphere called Earth, I find myself enraptured with the wonder of the scenic and natural beauty surrounding me. Planet Earth is one of a kind and deserves to be appreciated for the unselfish sharing of her grandeur.

♥ **AFFIRMATION** ♥

"Sweet Spirit, allow my heart to embrace the wonder of life on Earth."

LOVE *is my only* MASTER

--- ❤ ---

MAGNETIC MENTAL POWER

It is the Spiritual Warrior's responsibility to monitor all thoughts passing through the conscious mind. One soul's prolonged consideration of human lack and limitation can cause detriment to the world at large. Thoughts possess a highly magnetic power. They attract to the soul the very substance of their contemplation.

❤   **AFFIRMATION**   ❤

**"I long to know Heaven on Earth,
therefore, I will focus my mind on love alone."**

LOVE *is my only* MASTER

161

---❤---

HUMAN CONNECTEDNESS

As a member of humanity, I am separate from no one, and from nothing that touches the lives of my human family. Every emotion and circumstance experienced by a member of my humanity is experienced by me. I am one with Spirit, and Spirit is one with every living soul.

❤ **AFFIRMATION** ❤

"I am connected to all that lives, I am One with all life."

LOVE *is my only* MASTER

162

---❤---

ENERGY ACCELERATION

A gradual shift in Planet Earth's cosmic location has exposed her to a state of accelerated energy. There no longer seems to be the same 24 hours in a day. The affect of this increased energy on human livings has ranged from heightened creativity and spirituality to mental and emotional confusion. By centering my mind on this influx of energy, I can visualize it, receive it through my crown chakra, and utilize it in a most positive way.

❤ **AFFIRMATION** ❤

"As above, so below."

LOVE *is my only* MASTER

Today
I plant the seed of...

EXPECTANCY

As I learn to trust the loving energy of Spirit, I cease to struggle with the ups and downs of physical life. As challenges arise in life, I simply turn within, always expecting Spirit to provide me, unfailingly, with the enlightened guidance I desire.

♥ **AFFIRMATION** ♥

**"By living in a state of perpetual expectancy,
I prepare myself to receive spiritual illumination."**

LOVE *is my only* MASTER

❤

EARTH STEWARDSHIP

For many thousands of years, the Earth Mother has given of Herself unselfishly in order to assist the evolution of humankind. Now, as her child, I must do all I can to assist her. Caring for my personal environment, planting and nurturing all types of living things as well as learning to recycle is an excellent beginning.

❤ **AFFIRMATION** ❤

"I am an Earth Steward, and the Mother's chances for survival increase as my consciousness increases."

LOVE *is my only* MASTER

165

—

♥

Today
I plant the seed of...

CALMNESS

On a daily basis I am confronted with situations that test my patience, and challenge my spiritual skills. Becoming flustered or angry causes me to scatter my personal energies in a manner that is counter-productive to the highest good of all concerned.

♥ **AFFIRMATION** ♥

"A state of inner calmness is my strongest ally in all situations that confront me."

LOVE *is my only* MASTER

Today
I plant the seed of…

MY UNIQUENESS

Though my DNA is encoded with the same racial and universal data as everyone else's, the way I spontaneously express myself is utterly unique. There is no one else quite like me, and there shall never be. I need to appreciate myself for my matchless qualities and my unparalleled representation of Holy Spirit on Earth.

♥　　**AFFIRMATION**　　♥

**"I am at my spiritual best
when I honor my uniqueness."**

LOVE *is my only* MASTER

♥

Today
I plant the seed of...

SELF-HEALING

An imbalance within my mind or soul will manifest as discomfort of disease within my body. Yet, I have the Spirit given ability to heal myself through the power of positive thought energy.

♥   **AFFIRMATION**   ♥

"Self-healing naturally follows as I step more fully into my Oneness with Indwelling Spirit."

LOVE *is my only* MASTER

168

♥

OPEN HEARTEDNESS

It has been said by the Great Master that I can only come as a child into the Kingdom of Heaven. This wisdom implies that I must respond to life with the open heart of a child, if I am to behold that which cannot be seen by physical eyes. Open heartedness is a state of being wherein I am offering and receiving love unceasingly.

♥   **AFFIRMATION**   ♥

"I now open my heart to give and receive the abundant blessings of Infinite Love."

LOVE *is my only* MASTER

Today
I plant the seed of...

GOING BEYOND KARMA

I realize that within this Universe the Law of Cause and Effect abides. Every student of truth learns this in their earliest studies. As I approach a more advanced level of spiritual understanding, I begin to perceive my ability to transcend karma. By the power of positive thought energy I can minimize the influence that Karma exerts over my life's journey.

♥   **AFFIRMATION**   ♥

"I am made in the image of love, and the power of love transcends all Universal Law."

LOVE *is my only* MASTER

───── ♥ ─────

Today
I plant the seed of...

SUPPORTIVE FRIENDSHIP

I have many friends, for many different reasons. Some are friends because we share similar ideas and philosophies. Others are friends of mine because we work or play together. The friends dearest to me are those who know my soul, as I know theirs and support my spiritual growth. These friends enrich my life, enhance my well-being and bless me with happiness.

♥ **AFFIRMATION** ♥

"Supportive friendships represent hallowed ground upon my spiritual path."

LOVE *is my only* MASTER

Today
I plant the seed of...

SIMPLE PLEASURES

In this period of high tech and state of the art living, it is easy to misplace my capacity for slowing down and enjoying life's simple pleasures. Frolicking in a pile of fallen leaves or baking cookies with friends and family are both examples of simple pleasures that allow me to reconnect with what is most basic and beautiful about life.

♥ **AFFIRMATION** ♥

**"The greatest truth in life
is the simplest to comprehend."**

LOVE *is my only* MASTER

Today
I plant the seed of...

ENDING PROCRASTINATION

As a Light Worker upon Planet Earth today, I find myself in a very unique position. The luxury of unlimited time is no longer mine. I cannot afford to put off until tomorrow what I need to do today. Every day I live, and through every action I take, I must be ever mindful of the Will of Heaven.

♥ ## AFFIRMATION ♥

"I will end procrastination for it serves to weaken my spiritual resolve."

LOVE *is my only* MASTER

♥

CONQUERING FEAR

In the presence of light no darkness can exist. As a Spiritual Warrior I can follow only one master. If love is my master and guiding light, fear has no power in my life except that which I give it.

♥ **AFFIRMATION** ♥

"I conquer my fears by focusing my mind on the Light of Spirit."

LOVE *is my only* MASTER

---❤️---

SPIRIT'S PLAN

As I look around myself, I cannot help but marvel at the intricacies and perfection of Spirit's handiwork. Because of the beauty I behold, I refuse to succumb to pessimism. In solitude and meditation, my heart speaks to me of the promise of the Infinite Love and Light awaiting this realm.

❤️ **AFFIRMATION** ❤️

**"As I go within, Holy Spirit
reveals to me its plan of perfection."**

LOVE *is my only* MASTER

♥

Today
I plant the seed of...

HONORING UNIVERSAL CYCLES

I am one with the All That Is. Therefore, it is my destiny to honor the universal cycles of change. If I should resist the occurance of life-cycles, I deplete my precious energy, and I am left feeling at odds with life. As I honor these cycles I am filled with flowing energy and a thirst for life well lived.

♥ **AFFIRMATION** ♥

"I allow my life to be perfected by the blessing flowing forth with each cosmic cycle of change."

LOVE *is my only* MASTER

176

Today
I plant the seed of...

LISTENING TO MY BODY

There are many demands placed upon the Light Workers. I have my own growth and evolution to nurture as well as my responsibilities to the greater family. When so much is happening, on a daily basis, it is quite easy for me to overlook my need for rest. I must learn to listen and respond to my body.

♥   **AFFIRMATION**   ♥

"Listening to my body is paramount to my success as a Light Worker."

LOVE *is my only* MASTER

Today
I plant the seed of...

MY POTENTIAL

I have been sent to Earth by the Universal Powers in order to expand my awareness, and magnify my potential for love. As a spark from the Mother-Father-God, I am capable of doing all things. However, my Earth assignment directs me to focus most fully on those things that by doing well, I bring to myself and the world greater joy.

♥ **AFFIRMATION** ♥

"I live up to my Infinite Potential by experiencing and spreading spiritual joy."

LOVE *is my only* MASTER

Today
I plant the seed of...

EXCITEMENT

I am living in one of the most exciting times of growth ever known on earth. All around me freedom is demanding its place in the world. Higher thought is finding its way into the world's music, art, and literature. More and more of my brothers and sisters are becoming inspired to commence their individual quests for peace of mind through spiritual understanding.

♥ **AFFIRMATION** ♥

"Holy One, I ask that you continually renew my spirit with Divine excitement."

LOVE *is my only* MASTER

♥

AFFIRMATIONS

Replacing old, self-limiting tapes, in my unconscious, with new, enlightened messages, is a vital exercise for the Spiritual Warrior. By affirming my greatest good as the outcome to every challenge I face, I elevate my conscious awareness of Spirit. I also elevate the frequency of the challenge so that it is no longer in conflict with my personal energy. By doing this, I also elevate the frequency of the challenge until it is no longer in conflict with my personal energy.

♥ **AFFIRMATION** ♥

"Affirmations are a magical key for transforming my world."

LOVE *is my only* MASTER

Today
I plant the seed of...

THE COSMIC MOTHER

I could never know myself in totality, without coming to know the Mother of one thousand names. The Supreme Feminine Power of the Cosmos has been known to every culture since time immemorial. She is the Blessed One on High, birthing Universes and bringing them to maturity through her Infinite Love and compassion. Her Spirit lives in every man, woman and child.

♥ **AFFIRMATION** ♥

"Great Mother, hold me close and guide me to the full knowledge of myself through our intimate association."

LOVE *is my only* MASTER

Today
I plant the seed of...

I Am

There is but One I Am and I am a part of its vast greatness. Like a single droplet dancing in the endless sea, I am one with the Infinite.

♥ **Affirmation** ♥

"I am, and what I am is pure love and light due to the Power and Presence of Spirit within me."

LOVE *is my only* MASTER

———————— ♥ ————————

BEING PERFECT

As a Light Worker, I have been sent from another world or dimension to assist the earth in her upliftment. It is part of my spiritual responsibility to manifest the perfection of the Holy Spirit on Earth.

♥ **AFFIRMATION** ♥

**"Mother-Father God, as an ambassador
in your sacred legion, I will proudly seek
to present your perfection in all I say and do."**

LOVE *is my only* MASTER

Today
I plant the seed of...

BEGINNER'S EYE

The beginner's eye is unclouded. As I behold the world around me, ever changing, ever new, I need to remember to see it through the beginner's eye. I cannot measure today by yesterday's standard. As each new day dawns, I am recreated. As I reach my zenith with the noon Sun, and unwind with its setting, I still must cleave to the beginner's eye within me, untainted and unprejudiced.

♥ **AFFIRMATION** ♥

"The beginner's eye is my passport into the Kingdom of Heaven."

LOVE *is my only* MASTER

Today
I plant the seed of...

DETACHED EMPATHY

Empathy is a divine quality longing to find its way into every human heart. However, by becoming attached to having empathy, oft times, I paralyze my ability to contribute healing to the person or situation in need. Empathy reflects my personal understandings of emotion. Detached empathy reaches beyond emotion, to the solutions found in the Heart of Spirit.

♥ ## AFFIRMATION ♥

"Detaching from emotion frees my soul to work spiritual miracles."

LOVE *is my only* MASTER

Today
I plant the seed of...

UNIVERSAL CONNECTEDNESS

As I aspire to ever greater levels of spiritual awareness, I gently come into a consciousness of Universal Connectedness. I am one with the sky and the moon. I am part of the ocean and the Earth. All life is energy, all energy is consciousness.

♥ **AFFIRMATION** ♥

"My consciousness expands to include the Infinite as I tap into my Universal Connection."

LOVE *is my only* MASTER

Today
I plant the seed of...

EXPERIENCING THE PAIN

It is the nature of the human living to think of interfering with life when it appears that pain and suffering are on the horizon. Yet, it is the wisdom of Spirit to allow the experience of pain to have its full expression, when and where it has been summoned.

♥   **AFFIRMATION**   ♥

**"I willfully experience the pain I have
attracted as I simultaneously affirm that
all future growth will be precipitated only by joy."**

LOVE *is my only* MASTER

Today
I plant the seed of...

LIVING IN THE PRESENCE

While I busy myself each day with the business of life in the physical realm, it is in my highest interest to maintain a conscious awareness of my Oneness with the Great I Am. All crooked places are made straight, and life is enchanted when I live in the awareness that it is in this Divine Presence that I live, move and have my being.

❤ **AFFIRMATION** ❤

**"Life is never more beautiful than
when I remember that I am living in
the I Am Presence of the God/dess Supreme."**

LOVE *is my only* MASTER

Today
I plant the seed of...

INFLUENCE

It is an integral part of my Earth assignment to make my loving and inspired influence felt. It is not enough for me to attain wisdom, and emotional mastery this time around. I must also endeavor to influence the lives of others in the most positive and constructive way possible.

♥ **AFFIRMATION** ♥

"My spiritual savvy must be used as an uplifting influence for the good of all."

LOVE *is my only* MASTER

♥

WHITE LIGHT INFUSION

Before I leave my bed each morning, I will close my eyes and contact the God-Mind deep within me. I will envision the White Light of the Upper Ray. Through my third eye, I will direct this light into every single cell of my being. In so doing, I infuse my physical life with the Infinite Life of Spirit.

♥ **AFFIRMATION** ♥

"Now and forevermore I am cradled in the sheltering arms of Eternal Love."

LOVE *is my only* MASTER

Today
I plant the seed of...

LIFTING THE LOAD OF THE WEARY

From time to time we all become overwhelmed with the stresses and workload of modern living. If I can, in any way, at any time, help lift the load from one of my weary brothers or sisters, then this I must do. Offering to watch the children of a tired parent, or running errands for a busy friend are little things that can make a big difference in someone else's life.

❤ **AFFIRMATION** ❤

"As a Spiritual Warrior, I am inwardly strengthened as I ease the burden of the weary."

LOVE *is my only* MASTER

Today
I plant the seed of…

BELIEVING IN MYSELF

Once I comprehend, at the deepest levels of my being, that I am the perfect manifestation of Godliness, I will automatically cease to doubt my worth. Accepting my identity as the physical counterpart of the Omnipotent One, I must believe in my power and greatness.

♥ **AFFIRMATION** ♥

"Believing in myself demonstrates my faith in the Mother-Father God."

LOVE *is my only* MASTER

Today
I plant the seed of...

COOPERATION

Working in harmony with my brothers and sisters on Earth is not always a joyful event, but I need to remember that it is a Holy One. We have all been hand picked to play on Spirit's team and personal discord does not serve the Will of Heaven.

♥ **AFFIRMATION** ♥

**"I bring joy to Heaven and Earth
as I learn to cooperate with Life."**

LOVE *is my only* MASTER

193

♥

Today
I plant the seed of...

RADIANT HEALTH

As a child of the Divine, I am to reflect the perfection of my Creator. My physical condition is one of the most obvious reflections of my spiritual state of being.

♥   **AFFIRMATION**   ♥

"I radiate perfect health."

LOVE *is my only* MASTER

❤

FAMILY

I was born into a family of souls who had much to teach me, much to give me and much to learn from me as well. It is not up to me to judge them for what I feel were their shortcomings. Being born into my family of choice was a select blessing and all that goes on within that family has been tailor-made to fit my level of evolution and understanding.

❤ **AFFIRMATION** ❤

"I owe a debt of gratitude to my original family, for without them I would not be who I am today."

LOVE *is my only* MASTER

───────────── ♥ ─────────────

WILLINGNESS

The physical realm is the launching pad into higher dimensions of thought and beingness. As a soul, venturing the path of perfection, I need to remind myself to demonstrate willingness at every turn. I must be willing to learn, even when every fiber within me resists.

♥   **AFFIRMATION**   ♥

**" I must be willing to love, even when
the thought of it seems impossible."**

LOVE *is my only* MASTER

196

Today
I plant the seed of...

THINKING SPIRITUALLY

What I do unto the least of my breathren, I do unto the Universal Heart. Every time I take an action, I need to think about the possible spiritual ramifications. Will my words and deeds contribute love and light, or fear and limitation, to this realm? Getting into the habit of thinking with my spiritual mind will increase my vibration and the vibration of Planet Earth.

♥ **AFFIRMATION** ♥

**"As I open my consciousness to
receive thoughts from Universal Mind,
I fill the Universal Heart with gladness."**

LOVE *is my only* MASTER

♥

THE JOY OF INTIMACY

Intimacy is the gift of love unconditionally reciprocated by two people. The sharing of intimate meals, conversations, and physical exchanges of affection are among some of the most beautiful elements of the human experience.

♥   **AFFIRMATION**   ♥

**"I cherish the joy of intimacy as
a treasured gift from the Goddess."**

LOVE *is my only* MASTER

198

Today
I plant the seed of...

Preparing Myself As A Vessel

Throughout lifetime after lifetime, my soul urge has been towards the attainment of truth and spiritual enlightenment. Finding the answers to the mysteries of life has been my driving force. Preparing to serve as a vessel of goodness has been my Holy mission.

♥ **Affirmation** ♥

**"It is my destiny to serve as a
vessel for the Light of Love."**

LOVE *is my only* MASTER

♥

Today
I plant the seed of...

LIGHT HEARTEDNESS

When my heart feels as if it will break, and my world seems like a house full of strangers, it is then that I need to fill my heart with the Light of Spirit. Light heartedness means embracing the Light of the Christos. Where there is light, no darkness of Spirit can remain.

♥ **AFFIRMATION** ♥

"I am the Light of the World."

LOVE *is my only* MASTER

Today
I plant the seed of...

GIVING OF MYSELF

Love is the Universal reality. In truth, it is the only real thing that exists. I am love and by giving of myself, I give love to the world.

♥ **AFFIRMATION** ♥

"Love is the only lasting gift that I can give."

LOVE *is my only* MASTER

Today
I plant the seed of...

AUTHENTIC HUMANITY

To become an authentic human, I must fully acknowledge my physical restrictions, while fully accentuating my spiritual perfection. In order to experience authentic humanity, I must not fear the tribulations of life and, I must not shun the ecstasies inherent in life on Earth. I must face life on its terms so that I can assist others in doing the same.

♥ **AFFIRMATION** ♥

"The authenticity of my humanness is measured by my courage to live and let live."

LOVE *is my only* MASTER

♥

Today
I plant the seed of...

ENJOYING LIFE

If I allow my mind to focus on natural catastrophies and global injustices, the beauty and pleasure that is also present in life will surely pass me by. The Earth has its share of problems, yet it offers me great enjoyment.

♥ **AFFIRMATION** ♥

"As I learn to think on beauty and love, my life attracts and reflects these Divine qualities."

LOVE *is my only* MASTER

Today
I plant the seed of...

HOLY EXPRESSION

I am a perfect thought of the Almighty. I carry within me the Light of Christ, the Love of Goddess and the Infinite Intelligence of God. My life is immortal, my Spirit invincible. It is my destiny to express my Divinity through a life lived in dedication to the righteous principles of the Holy Spirit.

♥   **AFFIRMATION**   ♥

"I am the holy expression of Spirit's perfection."

LOVE *is my only* MASTER

♥

PUTTING THE PAST TO REST

All of my yesterdays have been packed with learning experiences and everlasting joys. As the future reaches out to embrace me, I will embrace the many happinesses I have earned, and will put away all sorrow, regret and unclaimed baggage.

♥ ## AFFIRMATION ♥

"Leaving behind disappointment and heartbreak, I step into all of my tomorrows with optimism, steadfastness and an open heart."

LOVE *is my only* MASTER

Today
I plant the seed of...

APPRECIATION

My blessings in life increase and multiply as as I begin to acknowledge them and give thanks accordingly. By living in a state of conscious appreciation, I create more and more to be thankful for.

❤ **AFFIRMATION** ❤

"Appreciation opens the door to my Divine Abundance."

LOVE *is my only* MASTER

206

♥

Today
I plant the seed of...

RADIATING MY DIVINE NATURE

The Universal Law of Attraction compells me to align my physical self with my Divine Reality. Like attracts like. As long as I radiate my Divine Nature in all my daily interchanges, it is law that I bring out the Divine in all the people and situations I encounter.

♥ **AFFIRMATION** ♥

**"In radiating my Divine Nature
I light the way for others to follow."**

LOVE *is my only* MASTER

207

Today
I plant the seed of...

NOT QUESTIONING WHY

The Divine Mind is so expansive, so limitless, that comprehension of it by the mortal mind is an impossible task. Therefore, the reason and purpose for every happening in the Universe is often beyond the scope of human understanding.

♥ **AFFIRMATION** ♥

"Learning to trust Infinite Intelligence is a sign of supreme spiritual wisdom."

LOVE *is my only* MASTER

♥

SEEING ONLY LOVE

Everything I perceive as reality was first a product of my own mind. I project my mental pictures and attitudes onto life's blank canvas, then I experience the results of these positive or negative thought energies.

♥ **AFFIRMATION** ♥

**"If I choose to see only love,
then love will become my only reality."**

LOVE *is my only* MASTER

209

♥

MY MAGNIFICENCE

I am flawless. I am the beautiful
reflection of my Divine parentage.
No matter what imperfection my
humanness portrays my identity as
spiritual perfection is unthreatened.
I am the essence of the Great I Am.

♥ **AFFIRMATION** ♥

**"I am the magnificent
expression of Universal Perfection."**

LOVE *is my only* MASTER

---❤️---

TAKING THE FIRST STEP

Often times in life, the only thing that stands between me and my greatest victory is the fear of taking that first step. Whether it is that diet I wish to begin, the new job I seek, or the pursuing of my dream of dreams, today I pledge to take the first step necessary. I will never know what I can accomplish if I am frozen in place by fear.

❤️ **AFFIRMATION** ❤️

"Today I will take the first step towards my innate greatness."

LOVE *is my only* MASTER

─────────────── ♥ ───────────────

DARING TO BE MYSELF

Within me there is a unique blue-print for a life purposefully lived. My mission on Earth is the rediscovery of unconditional love and the meaning of Infinite Life. As such, I must dare to be true to myself. I must follow my inner guidance no matter where it leads.

♥ **AFFIRMATION** ♥

"I manifest the power of Infinite Spirit when I dare to be myself."

LOVE *is my only* MASTER

Today
I plant the seed of...

CREATING A LIFE OF LOVE

I am the creative force at the center of my personal universe. Everything that transpires in my world is a direct response to my dominant thoughts and actions. My desire to create a life of love dictates that I recreate my world of thoughts and emotions.

♥ **AFFIRMATION** ♥

"From this day forward, I will give energy to only those thoughts and emotions which empower love and harmony in my life."

LOVE *is my only* MASTER

Today
I plant the seed of...

EXERCISING MY THIRD EYE

As I unfold to my spiritual nature, learning to see without my physical eyes is imperative. First I need to see myself through my spiritual eyes, then I can behold the spiritual essence of the world around me. So, for my first exercise: periodically, throughout the day, I shall close my eyes and behold my inbeing clothed in the Seven Rays of Divine Realization.

♥ **AFFIRMATION** ♥

"I love and appreciate myself more fully as I view my reality through the clarity of my third eye."

LOVE *is my only* MASTER

---------- ♥ ----------

Today
I plant the seed of...

SPIRITUAL RENEWAL

This is a perfect day to renew my spirit. If I allow myself to spend time in contemplation of spiritual matters, I will surely find myself renewed. Reflecting on my true nature as a child of Infinite Love acts to strengthen and inspire me. Time spent in deep meditation, today, will enable me to focus my thoughts and energies in the days ahead.

♥　　　**AFFIRMATION**　　　♥

"I am spiritually renewed by time sitting quietly in the I Am Presence."

LOVE *is my only* MASTER

---♥---

Today
I plant the seed of...

LIVING IN AN AWAKENED STATE

Mastering the arts of prayer, meditation and surrender are necessary steps to be taken towards my awakening. Through the use of these three Divine skills, I am enabled, every moment of everyday, to remain in an awakened state of spiritual consciousness. I cannot turn back, and I cannot allow myself to lapse into the sleep of ignorance , ever again.

♥ **AFFIRMATION** ♥

**"Becoming aware was facile;
maintaining a fully awakened state,
as I soujourn the Valley of Shadows is my true test."**

LOVE *is my only* MASTER

♥

DELIBERATION

When I speak and act in haste, I am more likely to experience remorse. However, when I deliberately pause long enough to draw upon the wisdom of the Goddess, I bring only honor and truth to myself and others.

♥   **AFFIRMATION**   ♥

"As I speak with the deliberation of love and wisdom, I manifest the Goddess within."

LOVE *is my only* MASTER

---❤---

Today
I plant the seed of...

Choosing To Be Joyful

I have the ability to choose to be joyful
regardless of what is going on around
me. Leftover problems and concerns
shall not disturb my inner joy, if that is
my conviction.

❤ **Affirmation** ❤

**"I am in control of my life
and today I choose to be joyful."**

LOVE _is my only_ MASTER

Today
I plant the seed of...

MY MINISTRY

Today, the Universe has placed me in a perfect position to do the Will of Heaven. My life is my ministry. The focus of my ministry is to bring the Golden Light of Love into focus anywhere and everywhere I find myself.

♥ **AFFIRMATION** ♥

"I pledge to minister to my brothers and sisters with love and kindness all the days of my life."

LOVE *is my only* MASTER

---❤---

UNLIMITING INFINITE MIND

Spirit desires that all my dreams come true. Happiness, health and abundance are indeed my Divine Inheritance. Yet my human mind constantly limits the full measure of my spiritual bounty. Through doubt and disbelief, I limit the outpouring of Infinite Mind's blessings into my life.

❤   **AFFIRMATION**   ❤

"In Infinite Mind every blessing is already mine."

LOVE *is my only* MASTER

Today
I plant the seed of...

BEING FULLY ALIVE

I will experience the fullness of my life to the extent that I allow myself the honest pleasure and passion of my being. By taking risks, seeking out new adventures and lovingly searching for the face of God in everyone I meet, I will come to intimately know the exhilaration of being fully alive.

♥ **AFFIRMATION** ♥

"I am fully alive when my passion is my purpose."

LOVE *is my only* MASTER

♥

ARTICULATING ALL GOODNESS

How naturally human it is for me to show interest in the sensational details of the nation's latest front page scandal. I know this kind of curiosity is essentially meaningless. Idle talk of such tragedy multiplies the suffering of those involved.

♥ **AFFIRMATION** ♥

"Sweet Spirit, give me eyes to see and a voice to articulate all the goodness that is taking place in our world today and everyday. "

LOVE *is my only* MASTER

Today
I plant the seed of...

STANDING UP AGAINST IGNORANCE

With open eyes, it is not difficult to see that hatred, racism and prejudice are reaching yet another peak in popularity. The media has fanned the flames of ignorance in hopes of exposing it; however, instead it appears to have given it license, in the small minds of many. As a teacher of the truth, it is my obligation to Loving Spirit to stand up against such ignorance, anywhere and in anyway I can.

♥ **AFFIRMATION** ♥

"The display of tolerance in the presence of hatred and racism acts to condone the most hideous of all human evils. "

LOVE *is my only* MASTER

Today
I plant the seed of...

DISSOLVING MY OBSTACLES TO PEACE

Infinite Spirit has guided my immortal soul to this land of discovery for many reasons. The presence of so-called obstacles, in my life, were designed in order to gently lead my heart on its quest for unconditional peace. As I allow myself to become more and more centered in this peacefulness, I find that obstacles dissolve before my very eyes.

♥ **AFFIRMATION** ♥

"Sweet Spirit, in my love for you I find peace without end."

LOVE *is my only* MASTER

224

---❤---

Today
I plant the seed of…

BEING LOYAL TO MY WORD

There have been times when I said something just because I thought it was what someone needed to hear. I didn't say it because it was heartfelt or because I planned to back it up with any real action. I simply wanted to stroke an ego or smooth some ruffled feathers. While this kind of behavior may be expeditious, it is not honest. It manifests no honor in my spoken word. By being loyal to my word I eliminate the need for a great many future apologies.

❤　　　**AFFIRMATION**　　　❤

"Every time I open my mouth, sweet Spirit, please help me utter only those words to which I can be loyal."

LOVE *is my only* MASTER

225

Today
I plant the seed of...

SOFTNESS

A soft voice and a gentle answer can calm almost any situation. It takes just as much precious time, and even more energy, to shout out a harsh reply. With the sincerity of the angels, and the sweetness of love, this day I will attempt to respond to every person and circumstance with softness. For with firmness to support it, the strength of softness is mightier than the sharpest sword.

♥　　　**AFFIRMATION**　　　♥

"I am made invincible by aligning myself with Spirit through the mystical Tao of softness."

LOVE *is my only* MASTER

Today
I plant the seed of...

REMEMBERING THE DEPARTED

There is a legacy of understanding and love left behind by each and every soul who ever walked the Earth. For no life was ever wasted. Every lesson ever mastered by a fellow soul, shines light on my life. Today I take time out to remember those loved ones who have ventured beyond this realm, yet have left behind a plethora of wit and wisdom from which I might draw a bit of strength and serenity.

♥ **AFFIRMATION** ♥

"Today I will contemplate the lives of those departed and I will be grateful for the priceless gifts that their lives have bequeathed me."

LOVE *is my only* MASTER

♥

EMOTIONAL SELF-PROTECTION

As I feel myself opening to the Universe, I more fully understand the concept of unconditional love and the relativity of physical reality. At the same time I must learn to accept the fact that everyone I meet will not share my exact philosophy. Opposing and diverse frequencies of thought will bombard my sacred space daily. Therefore, I shall not leave myself vulnerable and emotionally unprotected.

♥ ## AFFIRMATION ♥

"Each day before I step into the outer world, I shall shield myself with the White Light of loving protection."

LOVE *is my only* MASTER

228

♥

Today
I plant the seed of...

THE ETERNAL

Deceiving appearances abound in this physical realm of shadows. What is real and lasting is not always obvious to the human eye. It is my responsibility to tear away the veil of mystery in order to catch a glimpse of the eternal. Truth remains forever. Love can never pass away. Spirit is Infinite. In these eternal constants I will place my faith and trust.

♥ **AFFIRMATION** ♥

"I am one with Eternal Love, Light and Life."

LOVE *is my only* MASTER

Today
I plant the seed of...

EXUBERANCE

In all the cosmos, there is positively nothing more thrilling than the presence of spiritual exuberance. While basking in the sparkle of this awesome quality one is magically transported to the heavenly kingdom. To emanate spiritual exuberance is to emulate the passionate nature of the Universal Creative Principle. In all ways, I will seek to bring exuberance to my life tasks, my personal being and my sacred space.

♥ **AFFIRMATION** ♥

"The power and glory of Spirit is evidenced in my exuberance for life."

LOVE *is my only* MASTER

Today
I plant the seed of...

RIGHTEOUSNESS

As I endeavor to live my life by the Golden Rule I aim my sights on a life of righteousness. In being equitable in all my dealings I show respect for the Will of Heaven. By attempting to do what is morally correct under any and all circumstances I pay homage to my spiritual lineage.

♥ **AFFIRMATION** ♥

"Righteousness is my spiritual path."

LOVE *is my only* MASTER

Today
I plant the seed of…

RETURNING TO MY SPIRITUAL ROOTS

It matters little into which ethnic or cultural group I was born. My true family is the Family of God. My spiritual roots travel deep into the reaches of time and space. They are not limited to a small division of land here on Earth. I am a cherished member of the Universal family. My family ties are cosmic and forever unbreakable.

♥ **AFFIRMATION** ♥

**"My spiritual roots bind me
eternally to the Oneness of all life."**

LOVE *is my only* MASTER

───────────── ♥ ─────────────

Today
I plant the seed of...

SEEING THE OTHER SIDE

So many arguments and friendship estrangements occur simply due to the fact that one fails to see the other side of things. Being trapped by my own feelings restricts me from perceiving the myriad of options available to me. I limit my own growth by stubbornly closing my heart to new and alternative possibilities in thought. To be truly wise is to be informed. I am not wise if I consider only a single point of view.

♥ **AFFIRMATION** ♥

**"Becoming a true visionary begins
by learning to see life from all sides."**

LOVE *is my only* MASTER

FOREGOING STRUGGLE

For this one day, I promise myself that no matter what conflict or inconvenience confronts me, I shall forego the inclination to struggle against it. I will flow with all situations in a mindful and fluid manner. I will stay attuned to the stress levels in my body, reminding myself to breathe deeply and release all tension swiftly. Sacrificing my need for struggle will free my mind and heart for more pleasurable activities.

♥ **AFFIRMATION** ♥

**"To struggle is human,
to forego struggle is Divine."**

LOVE *is my only* MASTER

♥

SELFISHNESS

In all my bold and caring attempts to contribute my share on behalf of my human family, I must not forget to nurture myself. Acts of selfishness, such as time alone, saying no when necessary, and asking for what I need, are imperative for a spiritual Light Worker. There will be times when I will only be able to nurture the world, by nurturing myself.

♥   **AFFIRMATION**   ♥

**"As I practice regular acts of selfishness,
I bathe my spirit in the splendor of self-love."**

LOVE *is my only* MASTER

♥

Today
I plant the seed of...

GENEROSITY

I enjoy many blessings in my life. The Universe is ever ready to grant my heartfelt wishes and support my loftiest dreams. For this reason, it is my great good fortune to share of myself with those souls who cross my path and touch my life. It blesses the entire Universe whenever I assist and inspire another soul upon their journey towards wholeness. The Spirit of Generosity is part of my Divine Inheritance.

♥ **AFFIRMATION** ♥

"To be generous with my time, energy and encouragement, on behalf of another, is to be faithful to my Indwelling Spirit of Love."

LOVE *is my only* MASTER

Today
I plant the seed of...

MY UNLIMITED POWER

When I was a very young child, the world seemed so vast yet so accessible. I imagined that I could learn to fly. I dreamed of discovering a cure for all disease and scale the highest mountain known to man. I now know that nothing is beyond my scope of vision. I believed that nothing was beyond my grasp.

♥   **AFFIRMATION**   ♥

"Miracles begin and end with the unlimited power of my imagination"

LOVE *is my only* MASTER

Today
I plant the seed of...

INTUITIVE GUIDANCE

It is so important that I allow my intuitive essence to guide me throughout the day. Yet, every petty thought I think, and each negative word I speak, stands as a barrier between me and my spiritual intuition. Gradually, with love, I need to reposition my intellect and release ego so that they no longer interfere with the loving issue of my intuitive guidance.

♥ **AFFIRMATION** ♥

"My intuition is the whispering Voice of Spirit."

LOVE *is my only* MASTER

Today
I plant the seed of...

BEING A BRINGER OF GLAD TIDINGS

Into each life, disappointment, loss and unhappiness find their way. I cannot allow any state of frustration to become a way of life for me. The appearance of a difficult circumstance is simply a temporary expression of a physical challenge brought on by spiritual myopia.

♥   **AFFIRMATION**   ♥

"As a Spiritual Warrior, it is my quest to be a bringer of glad tidings into a world too often colored with sorrow."

LOVE *is my only* MASTER

Today
I plant the seed of...

SHARING MY LOVE

In order for me to fully comprehend my spiritual nature, I must begin to experience the full force of the loving power within. Sharing my love with those who share my life, my path and my vision is part of my destiny. I share my love by patiently giving of my heart and soul in whatever way suits the life event at hand.

♥ **AFFIRMATION** ♥

"The Love of Spirit is ceaseless and unending; the more I share my love, the more I have to share."

LOVE *is my only* MASTER

---- ♥ ----

Today
I plant the seed of...

BANISHING WORRY

If I truly comprehend that within the Universe there is only One Loving Spirit, One Unlimited Source, dedicated to my happiness and well-being, then why do I so often give way to worry? Worry is nothing more than doubt. Doubt is a direct lack of faith. Furthermore, over time, worry's personal vibration will erect a very tall wall between me and my Highest Good.

♥ **AFFIRMATION** ♥

"This day I shall replace all worrisome thoughts with seeds of faith planted firmly in the fertile soil of Infinite Supply."

LOVE *is my only* MASTER

241

COMMUNICATING WITH THE INFINITE

Within my being there dwells the essence and presence of Supreme Perfection. I am part of All That Is. I have the precious ability to communicate with the Infinite by stilling my mind through meditation and by opening my heart through the purifying Light of Love.

❤   **AFFIRMATION**   ❤

"At all times, Infinite Mind stands ready and willing to commune with my Spirit."

LOVE *is my only* MASTER

Today
I plant the seed of...

PENETRATING THE VEIL OF WICKEDNESS

If ever I should become a target of hateful lies and viciousness, I must remain unshaken. Another's evil attack is nothing more than a display of self-loathing. The measure of one's wickedness is always manifested in direct proportion to their internal pain.

❤ **AFFIRMATION** ❤

"In the presence of wickedness I shall perceive the underlying pain, and react with compassion."

LOVE *is my only* MASTER

243

ENHANCING MY EARTHLY EXPERIENCE

I know that my life has purpose and meaning. I arrived on Earth with a great and wondrous spiritual plan for the promotion of my personal evolution through the contribution of my God-given talents. I must use these talents for the benefit of all humankind. I enhance the pleasure of my Earthly experience by giving back to the world as much as I receive from Spirit.

❤ **AFFIRMATION** ❤

"My life is enhanced by all the love and joy I manage to give away."

LOVE *is my only* MASTER

♥

MY RESURRECTION

Life is Eternal. Death is not a reality, life cannot be annihilated. The symbology of resurrection is used to instruct us that no matter how long we have been asleep, (unconscious to the truth of Divine Spirit) we can rise again. Our lives can become holy instruments of love, once we grasp our Oneness with the Infinite.

♥ **AFFIRMATION** ♥

"I am resurrected by my conscious acceptance of my Oneness with Divine Spirit."

LOVE *is my only* MASTER

Today
I plant the seed of...

ACCENTING THE POSITIVE

There are so many marvelous people and things in my life that deserve celebrating. I cannot allow myself to ever get stuck in neutral because everything is not going along according to my will. It is the Will of Heaven that I long to serve. And I do that best by accenting the positive that resides in each and every moment I live.

❤ **AFFIRMATION** ❤

"My positive outlook is a loving tribute to the Great Cosmic Mother."

LOVE *is my only* MASTER

♥

Today
I plant the seed of...

SEEKING OUT LIKE MINDS

It is such a joy to find like minds with which to share my spiritual philosophies. In the exulted presence of Higher Thought my soul takes flight. I am elevated to new heights of inspiration when I surround myself, on a regular basis, with other souls dedicated to the pursuit of truth and enlightenment.

♥   **AFFIRMATION**   ♥

"Loving Spirit, lead me, this
day to kindred souls of like mind."

LOVE *is my only* MASTER

Today
I plant the seed of...

FINDING HARMONY AMID CHAOS

So often in life, things seem to get out of control. Life becomes too hectic as if the outer demands will never cease. In these times, it is imperative that I turn within to seek the harmony at the center of my being. Amid all outer chaos, there is peace within. Instead of struggling in the abyss of confusion, I need to train myself to go, automatically, to this sacred space, in times of disequilibrium.

♥ **AFFIRMATION** ♥

**"As I flounder in chaos I create
more of the same, therefore,
I turn within to bathe myself in God peace."**

LOVE *is my only* MASTER

---- ♥ ----

MAINTAINING MY TEMPLE

My physical body is my spiritual vehicle. The foods I feed it need to be alive in order to nourish my living temple. The thoughts I think about my body must be positive in order to support its optimum functioning. The exercise I give it must be regular and enjoyable in order for my body to benefit. The rest I offer my body must be peaceful and consistent so that internal order is preserved. Maintaining my temple is a serious responsibility.

♥   **AFFIRMATION**   ♥

"The quality of my spiritual life depends, in great part, upon how I maintain my temple."

LOVE *is my only* MASTER

Today
I plant the seed of...

PROSPERITY'S SPIRITUAL NATURE

As I pay attention to those around me, often I hear them expressing that money is not a spiritual thing to possess, and that people who have abundant income are somehow less spiritual than those still struggling with finances. This is a false and dangerous concept. For me, to live a prosperous and abundant life is the Will of Heaven. There is nothing spiritual about living in a consciousness of lack and limitation.

❤　　　**AFFIRMATION**　　　❤

"I know that I have reached spiritual maturity when I possess abundant good health, happiness and financial prosperity."

LOVE *is my only* MASTER

TAPPING INTO UNIVERSAL MIND

Anyone who is capable of seeing into the future or the past is doing this by tapping into the Universal Mind. It would seem that psychics and sensitives have a direct line to God, yet, this line is accessible to me as well. By acknowledging that there is only One Universal Mind and that I am part of it, I can learn to connect with the Universe at will. All knowledge and information, meaningful to me, is available if only I seek to find it.

♥ **AFFIRMATION** ♥

"As my Spirit seeks Oneness with the Holy Spirit, through prayer and meditation, my mind automatically finds Oneness with the Universal Mind."

LOVE *is my only* MASTER

251

STANDING ON FAITH

At times I feel I have done all I can to reach my spiritual goals, and still, I've come up short. Life simply is not what I want it to be. It seems, that with all I have studied and all I've tried, I am not living the spiritual life I long for. Well, the good news is that everyone goes through these phases of feeling "Spiritually Stagnant." During these periods I must stand on faith, knowing steadfastly that my sincere efforts will manifest richly in the right and perfect time.

❤ **AFFIRMATION** ❤

"The Depth and measure of my faith will determine the bounty of my spiritual life."

LOVE *is my only* MASTER

———————— ♥ ————————

Today
I plant the seed of...

MY TIMELESSNESS

The number of birthdays that I have to celebrate are not an accurate indicator of my age. As a Child of Light I am ageless. Forever is my time frame. I will remain as young as my mental outlook. I need never feel old if I constantly rejuvenate myself by embracing only thoughts of my vitality and youth.

♥   **AFFIRMATION**   ♥

"I am a beautiful reflection of the timelessness of eternal life."

LOVE *is my only* MASTER

253

Today
I plant the seed of...

DEDICATING EACH DAY TO GOD

Before rising from bed each morning it would serve me well to take a moment to dedicate the upcoming day to the service of the Mother-Father God. In their presence and according to their will, I shall step into my day and do all that is possible to bring Divine Light and Love to my corner of the world.

♥   **AFFIRMATION**   ♥

"At the beginning of each new day I dedicate myself to the service of love and light."

LOVE *is my only* MASTER

♥

Today
I plant the seed of...

SPONTANEITY

Life is meant to be lived with spontaneous zest and vigor. But, being a spontaneous Spirit is not always easy. I have to teach myself to act with spontaneity. Physical life has conditioned me to think before I speak and look before I leap. When I seek Oneness with Infinite Thought and open my heart to unconditional love, I need not fear the results of my spontaneity.

♥ **AFFIRMATION** ♥

"The spontaneous reactions of my Spirit are loving and inspired."

LOVE *is my only* MASTER

255

Today
I plant the seed of...

OVERCOMING INERTIA

God helps those who help themselves. I think I am being spiritual when I tell myself that if I wait patiently long enough, the Universe will resolve all my problems. This may be true. Still in all, there are many things that Spirit wants me to do to get the ball rolling in order to overcome my physical inertia and to signal Heaven that I am indeed seriously ready for action.

♥ **AFFIRMATION** ♥

"Sitting on my hands, waiting for Spirit to always take the lead, is not the way to victory for the Spiritual Warrior."

LOVE *is my only* MASTER

256

Today
I plant the seed of...

BEING CENTERED IN HAPPINESS

If I center myself in happiness each day, I will be more likely to see the joy and pleasure being offered me through all people and situations I encounter. Being centered in happiness becomes a snap once I am ever mindful that my anchor in life is the bliss found in the power and the presence of the Living Spirit.

♥ **AFFIRMATION** ♥

"When I anchor my soul in Spirit's love, my life becomes centered in true happiness."

LOVE *is my only* MASTER

♥

Today
I plant the seed of…

MY SPIRITUAL EDUCATION

When I first set out upon my spiritual
journey in search of Divine Truth, I was
taught to believe in that which I could
not see. Now, I am learning to see that
which is not visible. My spiritual educa-
tion is a lifetime commitment. I must
become comfortable with the fact that
I am always at my beginning.

♥ **AFFIRMATION** ♥

**"The more I learn, the more I realize that
there is no end to my spiritual quest for Truth."**

LOVE *is my only* MASTER

258

Today
I plant the seed of...

INTER-DIMENSIONAL LIVING

For many Children of Light, life is lived on more than one plane of existence or within more than one dimension. Life in the third dimension is very familiar and satisfactory for most people. For me, striving for At-One-Ment with the Holy Spirit dictates that I reach continually for higher levels of Infinite Reality. As I increase my level of awareness I quickly move into higher dimensions of being.

❤　　　## AFFIRMATION　　　❤

"Inter-dimensional living grants me a more holistic perspective of the supreme meaning and mystery of life."

LOVE *is my only* MASTER

Today
I plant the seed of…

MAKING CHECKLISTS

A sense of order and accomplishment are essential to the maintenance of physical and spiritual self-esteem. Making checklists is a wonderful way for me to bring order into my daily life. First I shall list all of those things I need to do. Then I shall list all the things I want to do. By combining the two lists, I can easily compile one list of all that is realistically possible for me to do, ending my day with an invigorating sense of accomplishment.

♥ **AFFIRMATION** ♥

**"Through the benefit of checklists,
Divine order is created in my life."**

LOVE *is my only* MASTER

--- ❤ ---

GRACEFUL BODY MOVEMENT

Graceful, fluid movements of the body are an excellent way to keep the flow of vital energy on track. In yoga or dance class, I can strengthen my spine, stamina and sense of serenity, through controlled, elegant body movements. I need to remember my physical body is an extension of my Spiritual body. Becoming physically attuned to the sway and undulations of the Universe affords deeper insight into the Cosmic Dance of Ecstasy.

❤   **AFFIRMATION**   ❤

"The beauty and splendor of the Goddess is witnessed in the graceful movements of the human body."

LOVE *is my only* MASTER

261

KEEPING MY EYES ON HEAVEN

Holy Spirit, there is so much to deal with in the world today. There is suffering, there is ignorance and there is lack of faith. I do my best to stay centered, loving and focused on Spirit. Yet, I ask your help to strengthen my resolve and to lift my, sometimes, heavy heart. In all that I do, let me do it for you, while keeping my eyes fixed on Heaven.

♥ **AFFIRMATION** ♥

"I easily fulfill my mission on Earth by keeping my consciousness focused on the Will of Heaven."

LOVE *is my only* MASTER

Today
I plant the seed of...

LOVING TRANSFORMATION

There is nothing on Earth or within my private life that I can change by hating it. Love is the only power for positive change. For love is the power of God. If I want to know true peace in my time, then first I must love peace into being. If I desire to know the ecstasy of Divine Love, then first I must give love away. All global and personal transformations must be precipitated by the power and presence of love.

♥ **AFFIRMATION** ♥

"The essence of my being and the seed of all transformation is love."

LOVE *is my only* MASTER

---------------- ♥ ----------------

EMBRACING MY TOTALITY

As I journey through this land of illusion, it is my task to remain ever mindful of embracing my totality. Because I am a Light Being, I cannot ignore the needs and desires of my physical mind and body. Though I am clad in human armor, I dare not forget my allegiance to my eternal reality as one with Spirit. Remaining conscious of my connection to both Heaven and Earth is my key to enlightenment.

♥   **AFFIRMATION**   ♥

"Today I embrace my totality and am made whole by celebrating all aspects of myself as Spirit in form."

LOVE *is my only* MASTER

---❤---

Today
I plant the seed of...

EXPERIENCING TRUTH

The Great Spirit does not wish for me to live my life on blind faith. Spirit commands that I challenge it. By asking for what I want, believing in my heart that it is already mine, and then witnessing its' manifestation in my life, I am given great reason to have a working faith in the Infinite. Universal truth can only become my personal truth after I have experienced it for myself.

❤ **AFFIRMATION** ❤

"My heart is purified and strengthened as I seek to make eternal truth my personal reality."

LOVE *is my only* MASTER

265

PERSONAL ACHIEVEMENT

There is a voice within telling me to "Get on with it." Now is the time for me to plant the seeds of my personal agenda. What do I want to achieve, just for me, this day? Where is it that I have always wanted to travel? Or what can I start saving for that I have always wanted to have? I must remember, that a thousand mile journey begins with the first step!

♥ AFFIRMATION ♥

"My personal achievements reflect the level of Divine Light that I have recognized within myself."

LOVE *is my only* MASTER

♥

ANONYMOUS GIVING

Imagine how thrilling it would be to receive a gift of genuine love from an anonymous giver. A simple note of encouragement, or a heartfelt poem reinforcing another's loveliness would surely bring unforgettable cheer to an otherwise ordinary day. Today I shall think of an original way to brighten the day of someone I know, as I brighten my own day with the joy of anonymous giving.

♥ **AFFIRMATION** ♥

"As I give of myself, without thought of compensation, I receive in return, beyond comprehension."

LOVE *is my only* MASTER

Today
I plant the seed of...

ESSENTIAL PURITY

If I truly comprehend that within the Universe there is only One Loving Spirit, One Unlimited Source, dedicated to my happiness and well-being, then why do I so often give way to worry? Worry is nothing more than doubt. Doubt is a direct lack of faith. Furthermore, over time, worry's personal vibration will erect a very tall wall between me and my Highest Good.

♥   **AFFIRMATION**   ♥

"My personal vibration is increased manifold by the purification of my thoughts and actions."

LOVE *is my only* MASTER

Today
I plant the seed of...

GLORIFYING MYSELF

At this moment, for better or worse, I am the sum total of everything I have ever thought, said or done. Yet above all else, I remain the image and glory of God. I live by the breath of the Goddess. I am the Spirit of Love. Any and all transgressions, over which I carry guilt, are nullified in the presence of Supreme Radiance. At any moment in time, I can dedicate my life to the glory of God/Goddess and I can begin again.

❤ **AFFIRMATION** ❤

**"By revering the glory that is mine,
I give glory to the God and Goddess."**

LOVE *is my only* MASTER

Today
I plant the seed of…

CELESTIAL MOTHER

She is the Universal Feminine Principle. The Celestial Mother is the Queen of Heaven and Earth. Every ancient civilization has suckled life from her breasts, and hailed her Divine. Today I will pay homage to her likeness in all women. On this day I will take time to acknowledge the magnificent contributions of all mothers to the survival, nurturance and upliftment of humankind.

❤ **AFFIRMATION** ❤

"I give thanks to the Celestial Mother for my life which is a gift of Her Divine Love."

LOVE *is my only* MASTER

♥

Today
I plant the seed of...

STABILIZING ENERGY

As a Light Bearer, I am also a healer. I have been beckoned to this realm to offer my unique brand of healing to Earth's inhabitants. One of the most important ways I help heal the planet is by stabilizing scattered or fluctuating energies. If I find myself in the presence of hostile or confused behavior, by refusing to be drawn in emotionally and concentrating mentally on a positive outcome, I can assist in stabilizing any negative or shifting energies.

♥   **AFFIRMATION**   ♥

"I can stabilize my unstable situation by holding a vision of its perfection in my mind."

LOVE *is my only* MASTER

271

Today
I plant the seed of...

TRANSCENDING PERSONALITIES

The Earth has often been referred to
as the University of Life. Of all the
courses offered here, the hardest to
ace is, transcending personalities.
Learning to go beyond the words and
deeds of kindred spirits, straight into
the soul and substance of their being,
can be most difficult. For many, lifetime after lifetime has been devoted
to the mastering of this one lesson.

♥   **AFFIRMATION**   ♥

**"Life's true value is witnessed through
the transforming power of relationships
and true relating can only happen soul to soul."**

LOVE *is my only* MASTER

Today
I plant the seed of...

BLESSING AND RELEASING

I have witnessed many of my brothers and sisters around me having to go without. There are homeless on the streets and families waving signs claiming they will work for food. If these unfortunate lives touch mine, I must act. I will give any food or money I can, asking Spirit to bless their lives as I have been blessed. Once I give of my own resources, and pray for Divine intervention, I must release the problem into Spirit's hands.

♥ **AFFIRMATION** ♥

"When the problem of another touches my heart, Spirit ask that I offer my support, raise my voice in prayer and then reflease my concern, in order for Spirit's love to flow unencumbered."

LOVE *is my only* MASTER

♥

FINDING DELIGHT IN THE MUNDANE

A bus ride to work, or mopping the kitchen floor are certainly not things that send a chill of excitement up my spine. Yet, these activities can be wrought with possibility. A bus ride could be the beginning of a special friendship. Mopping the floor could be time for fantasy or a solemn time for meditation. The point is I must open my mind to allow each mundane event to introduce its own unique brand of delight into my realm.

♥ **AFFIRMATION** ♥

"Each moment and every task in life has been designed for my pleasure and purpose."

LOVE *is my only* MASTER

274

Today
I plant the seed of...

ALLOWING MY JOY TO SHINE FORTH

Joy is the natural state of Spirit. With eyes to see, it is obvious that every small child and creature alike, are intrinsically blessed with the Spirit of joy and happiness. Joy is my Divine Inheritance.

♥ **AFFIRMATION** ♥

"I will allow the joy of my being to shine forth as a beacon of love for all to see."

LOVE *is my only* MASTER

LOVING MY NEIGHBOR

The Beloved Master told us to, "Love thy neighbor as thyself." What better time to reach out and touch my neighbor. There are no mistakes in the Universe, so my neighbors were placed beside me for a reason. Today I will introduce myself to a neighbor I've never met or perhaps, I could invite my neighbor in for tea. Any sincere offer of love to my neighbor will make a huge contribution to the well-being of the entire planet.

♥ **AFFIRMATION** ♥

"By initiating an atmosphere of friendship in my small neighborhood, I am shining the Light of Christ into every corner of the world."

LOVE *is my only* MASTER

---❤---

RITUAL

The act of performing rituals, as a means of deeply penetrating and impressing the conscious and unconscious minds, has been employed by every great and powerful civilization. In my private world, performing rituals helps to focus my energies and brings a sense of spiritual tradition and order to my life. Whether I ritualize my morning coffee, or light candles beside my evening bath, these regular ceremonies are a form of worship.

❤ **AFFIRMATION** ❤

"Through perfecting the art of ritual I open my beingness to the power of the Universal forces within and round me."

LOVE *is my only* MASTER

Today
I plant the seed of...

RECORDING MY DREAMS

Dreamtime is a sacred creation of Infinite Mind designed to convey the whispers of wisdom from the Great Spirit to the souls of Earth below. During dreamtime I can receive inspired answers to lingering questions, and detailed descriptions of my future quest. Dreamtime demands my respect and offers me the greatest treasures of Heaven and Earth.

♥　　　## AFFIRMATION　　　♥

**"I will record my dreams and
witness a picturesque chronicle of my
Higher Life evolve before my very eyes."**

LOVE *is my only* MASTER

Today
I plant the seed of...

RELINQUISHING REGRET

Looking over my life, it is easy to recall many times when my behavior fell short of the spiritual ideal. I acted out of fear instead of faith, or I was grasping rather than trusting. There were also times when I sought to get even in lieu of reaching for understanding. But the point is that I recognize my errors in judgement, and I relinquish the regret which will only impede my spiritual advancement.

♥   **AFFIRMATION**   ♥

"In reality there are no right and wrong steps to Spiritual Mastery, there is only now and later."

LOVE *is my only* MASTER

Today
I plant the seed of...

HEALING MY LIFE

Though sickness may appear to invade my body, total health is my reality. At those times when I haven't two quarters for a cup a coffee, my true supply is unlimited. When I see no light at the end of the tunnel, I am illuminated from within by the Holy Spirit. I can heal all appearances in my life by consciously acknowledging, on every level of my being, the Presence and Perfection of God.

♥   **AFFIRMATION**   ♥

"I am instantly healed of all external effects by shifting my consciousness to the perfection of God."

LOVE *is my only* MASTER

Today
I plant the seed of...

CARING FOR MOTHER EARTH

Mother Earth is the shelter of my soul. She gives her energy so that I might share her life. It is up to me to give in return so that we both can survive. By planting a garden of vegetables or flowers I bring great happiness to the Earth and her elementals. Simply buying and nurturing a new house plant, today, will contribute to the quality of life on this splendid orb.

♥   **AFFIRMATION**   ♥

"I care for the Earth by respecting her as a living consciousness in need of loving attention."

LOVE *is my only* MASTER

CAPTURING THE DAY

Today is unlike any day that has ever been or will ever be again. Today I can see with brand new eyes, or wear a new attitude, if I choose. It matters not what happened to me yesterday, and tomorrow is but a dream. Let me revel in the inherent joy of this moment in time while I savor the once in a lifetime deliciousness of being totally in the adventure of this day.

❤ **AFFIRMATION** ❤

"Today will never come again, therefore, I shall open my heart to capture all the joy and wisdom it so lovingly longs to share."

LOVE *is my only* MASTER

Today
I plant the seed of...

WITHHOLDING OPINION

Because mine is a finite mind, I have not the capacity to understand the unlimited possibilities of energies at play in any given situation. What may present itself as a pretty cut and dried occurrence, in the physical, may be infinitely more complex in the spiritual scheme of things. A mind cluttered with endless opinions has little room to grasp the true meaning of life.

♥   **AFFIRMATION**   ♥

**"I can appreciate the miracle of life
when I learn to withhold all opinions."**

LOVE *is my only* MASTER

Today
I plant the seed of...

IMAGINEERING

It is a metaphysical fact that my thoughts create reality. This is the art of imagineering. Anything that I hold in my mind, and accept as real, must be made manifest in time. By holding the image of my future as bright and successful, I am actually commanding the Cosmic Forces of Light and Victory do do my bidding.

❤ **AFFIRMATION** ❤

**"Through the power and practice of imagineering,
I will attract to myself all that I desire."**

LOVE *is my only* MASTER

KEEPING IN TOUCH

Dropping a quick note to a friend I haven't seen in a while is an endearing way of telling them that they truly matter to me. Keeping in touch with short and long distance family augments that blessed sense of belonging. Feelings of love and closeness are nurtured by simple and easy acts of reaching out with the intention of connecting with someone, heart to heart.

♥ **AFFIRMATION** ♥

"I encircle my life with a song of unending love by keeping in touch with those near and dear to my heart."

LOVE *is my only* MASTER

---❤---

ASSUMING PERSONAL RESPONSIBILITY

The Mother-Father God has given me life, yet, I am co-creator with them. I am totally responsible for how I use or abuse my precious powers. The outer circumstances of my life are the fruits harvested from my inner visions. If I don't like something about my life, it is my responsibility to make the necessary changes in order to bring about the desired results.

❤ **AFFIRMATION** ❤

" I now assume sole responsibility for my happiness ."

LOVE *is my only* MASTER

Today
I plant the seed of...

KNOWING SPIRIT

So many times in a single day I become confused as to whether I am receiving messages from Spirit or from my ego mind. I feel that it is often impossible for me to know the difference, yet, as quickly as that thought passes another thought enters, saying, "Be still, and know." Spirit's identity is unmistakable. Spirit's power and presence is undeniable.

♥ **AFFIRMATION** ♥

**"I will still my thinking mind and
I will know, without a doubt, when
the voice of Spirit sweetly whispers my name."**

LOVE *is my only* MASTER

PROJECTING MY POWER

I was conceived in the image of God. Like the Infinite, I am powerful. Like the Universe, I am unlimited. I came to Earth to use my powers for good. I have come to display my likeness to God. Hiding my light under the proverbial bushel glorifies no one. To hide my likeness of love and light is indeed an insult against the Holy Spirit.

♥ **AFFIRMATION** ♥

"I project my power into the world so that it may multiply, touching the lives of many."

LOVE *is my only* MASTER

---- ♥ ----

SELF-ACCEPTANCE

No one is as critical of me as I am of myself. Of course, no one spends as much time looking for my faults, as I do. Deep in my heart, I know that I am exactly the way I was intended to be. If my arms are a little long, that's okay, for I can give a better hug. If I am a little short, so be it, for I get to stand closer to the hearts of others.

♥ **AFFIRMATION** ♥

**"My heart center bursts with unconditional love
for the world, as I learn to accept myself, exactly as I am."**

LOVE *is my only* MASTER

Today
I plant the seed of...

SEEKING TRUE LOVE

Every single one of us on Earth today longs to know "true love". Unfortunately, there are as many definitions for the meaning of "true love" as there are people seeking to find it. True love can only be found in my holy relationship to the Indwelling God. For this is the purest, simplest and most enduring power in the Universe. True love of God and self is the only love worth seeking, for once I find it all other treasures of the Heavenly Kingdom lie within my reach.

♥ **AFFIRMATION** ♥

"Once my heart has been touched by the ecstasy of Holy Love, I will need never seek again."

LOVE *is my only* MASTER

Today
I plant the seed of...

STUDYING NATURE

Hermes said, "As above so below, as below so above." Quite simply, he is telling us that every major cosmic drama is played out in miniature here on Earth. By studying the spontaneous unfoldment of life in nature, I can observe the Eternal Wisdom of the cosmos. Long before the advent of books and weekend seminars, the Wise Ones relied on the life of nature to reveal the mysteries of life within the human soul.

♥   **AFFIRMATION**   ♥

"The key to self-understanding can be found in the study of nature."

LOVE *is my only* MASTER

♥

RETREAT

Despite all my efforts to remain positive
and protected from outside negativity,
there are times when I simply feel a
tremendous need to be totally alone.
Solitude is often the only means of
recentering my scattered self. With
special attention to diet, meditation
and relaxation, I emerge form my
retreat recharged and more loving.

♥ ### AFFIRMATION ♥

**"I enter the Kingdom of Heaven
when I retreat in solitude."**

LOVE *is my only* MASTER

♥

Today
I plant the seed of...

SLOWING DOWN

Too often I find myself rushing about thinking only of my destination, without taking time to enjoy the journey. To be in the now means that I seize the uniqueness of this very instant, without giving thought to where I have just been or where I need to be shortly. By slowing down enough to experience the sights and smells around me, my mind is more anchored in the present. By remembering to breathe deeply, my being is firmly connected to the moment.

♥ **AFFIRMATION** ♥

**"Slowing down my physical pace
gives my senses a chance to absorb the
resplendent joy found in living one moment at a time."**

LOVE *is my only* MASTER

---❤---

*Today
I plant the seed of…*

DISCIPLESHIP

My spiritual beliefs ask that I follow a
path of goodness and live a life of love.
Being dedicated to that end is the
heart and soul of my mission on Earth.

❤ **AFFIRMATION** ❤

"I am a Spiritual Disciple, love is my only master."

LOVE *is my only* MASTER

About The Author

Kathryn M. Peters is an ordained minister, spiritual teacher and intuitive counselor. From her earliest memories Kathryn can recall being visited by angels compelling her to seek out Divine Love in a world of indifference. The self-realization of her uniqueness caused Kathryn to investigate many different religions and spiritual practices from around the world. This personal quest for spiritual identity led Kathryn to study the art of Astrology. Many answers to the Great Mysteries of Life were revealed to her through gaining an attunement to the Will of Heaven.

Once Kathryn felt a substantial degree of personal wholeness and Spiritual balance, she then was Divinely guided to open herself to assist others who were seeking the Light of Spirit. Her dedication towards the upliftment of those she meets is one of her primary joys in life.

Kathryn believes that we are all capable of enriching our lives and becoming successful human beings, fully loved and prosperous if only we can allow a realization of the Divine Presence within.

Love Is My Only Master comes as a result of her desire to help others realize the Eternal Truths residing within their hearts. This book is meant to uplift and help us to recall our Divine Nature.

Kathryn has been married to, James, her husband for over 20 years. They share their love and lives with their six beautiful children in Fallon, Nevada.

To contact Kathryn Peters, to order more books or to be placed on her mailing list write:

HeartLight Productions
2161 W. Williams
Suite 236
Fallon, NV 89406

---♥---

Have

a

Good

Destiny